PROJECT AIR FORCE

T0294826

Addressing Barriers to Female Officer Retention in the Air Force

Kirsten M. Keller, Kimberly Curry Hall, Miriam Matthews,

Leslie Adrienne Payne, Lisa Saum-Manning, Douglas Yeung,

David Schulker, Stefan Zavislan, Nelson Lim

Prepared for the United States Air Force

Approved for public release; distribution unlimited

For more information on this publication, visit www.rand.org/t/RR2073

Library of Congress Cataloging-in-Publication Data is available for this publication.
ISBN: 978-0-8330-9878-8

Published by the RAND Corporation, Santa Monica, Calif.
© Copyright 2018 RAND Corporation
RAND® is a registered trademark.

Cover: U.S. Air Force photo by Staff Sgt. Joe W. McFadden.

Support RAND
Make a tax-deductible charitable contribution at
www.rand.org/giving/contribute

www.rand.org

Preface

Women are underrepresented among the Air Force's senior leadership compared with their representation among the lower ranks. One factor contributing to this underrepresentation is that women tend to leave the active duty Air Force at higher rates than men. This report documents the results of a qualitative study designed to better understand the factors that female Air Force officers consider when deciding whether to remain in or separate from the active duty Air Force. The study conducted a total of 54 focus groups with 295 female Air Force officers in the spring of 2016 from across 12 different Air Force installations. The report describes the key retention factors identified through these focus groups and provides recommendations for improving Air Force policies and programs to help address potential barriers and improve female officer retention.

This research was cosponsored by the Office of the Assistant Secretary of the Air Force for Manpower and Reserve Affairs (SAF/MR) and the Air Force Deputy Chief of Staff for Manpower, Personnel and Services (AF/A1). It was conducted within the Manpower, Personnel, and Training Program of RAND Project AIR FORCE as part of a fiscal year 2016 study looking at improving diversity within the Air Force.

RAND Project AIR FORCE

RAND Project AIR FORCE (PAF), a division of the RAND Corporation, is the U.S. Air Force's federally funded research and development center for studies and analyses. PAF provides the Air Force with independent analyses of policy alternatives affecting the development, employment, combat readiness, and support of current and future air, space, and cyber forces. Research is conducted in four programs: Force Modernization and Employment; Manpower, Personnel, and Training; Resource Management; and Strategy and Doctrine. The research reported here was prepared under contract FA7014-16-D-1000.

Additional information about PAF is available on our website: www.rand.org/paf/

This report documents work originally shared with the U.S. Air Force in September 2016. The draft report, also issued in September 2016, was reviewed by formal peer reviewers and U.S. Air Force subject-matter experts.

Contents

Figures and Tables

Figures

Tables

Summary

With a focus on the potential value of diversity for improving innovation, agility, and ultimately the mission, the U.S. armed forces has long worked toward improving demographic representation within its ranks, including the representation of women (see Lucas and Segal, 2012). In the Air Force, Chief of Staff Gen David L. Goldfein has stated that, "Recruiting and retaining diverse Airmen cultivates innovation. Like different aircraft and missions make up one Air Tasking Order, different people make the best teams when integrated purposefully together" (U.S. Air Force, undated). To this end, starting in March 2015, the Air Force implemented a series of initiatives to try to improve diversity, including female representation within its ranks (see Secretary of the U.S. Air Force, 2015a; 2015b; 2016).

When it comes to improving female representation in the officer corps, military personnel statistics have shown a pattern for many years in which female officers in all services are generally less likely to progress through career milestones at the same rates as male officers. One consequence of this pattern is low female representation at the highest levels of leadership. In the Air Force, female officers currently make up 21.1 percent of officers in pay grades O-1 (second lieutenant) through O-5 (lieutenant colonel), but only 13.9 percent of officers at the O-6 level, and only 7.5 percent of officers at brigadier general (O-7) or higher.[1] In addition to promotion-related differences, research finds that persistent differences in retention are an important driver of the differences in officer career progression for men and women in the Air Force and military services more broadly (Asch, Miller, and Malchiodi, 2012; Hosek et al., 2001; Lim et al., 2014).

Figure S.1 illustrates the gender differences in retention for Air Force officers by showing cumulative continuation rates (CCRs) of Air Force personnel; the CCR for each commissioned year of service (CYOS) represents the average rate of continuation through that year and all previous years.[2] Due to differences in the length of initial active duty service commitments, the figure depicts the CCRs separately for rated or flying related occupations and nonrated occupations.[3] Most Air Force officer occupations require a four-year active duty service

---

[1] Based on RAND analyses of Air Force personnel data for August 2016 provided to RAND by the Air Force Personnel Center.

[2] CCRs are based on our calculations from FYs 2001–2015 Air Force personnel data. To form the CCRs, we first calculated the percentage of officers in each CYOS who remained through the next CYOS. Then, we multiplied these CYOS-specific continuation rates to form the CCR curves. The CCR for each CYOS, then, is the average rate of continuation through that year and all previous years. For example, the CCR for CYOS 2 is the percentage of all officers who remained through their first and second year of service, while the CCR for CYOS 20 is the percentage of officers retained through 20 years of service. We were not able to separate out individuals who left because of involuntary downsizing.

[3] Rated occupations include flying-related positions, such as pilot, navigator, combat systems officer, Air Battle Manager. Nonrated occupations are those that are not flying-related positions.

commitment. However, pilots make a ten-year active duty service commitment, and both Combat System Officers and Air Battle Managers make a six-year active duty service commitment. As expected, officers in rated occupations have higher CCRs in general because they tend to have a longer initial service commitment. However, female officers tend to have lower overall continuation rates than male officers in both rated and nonrated occupations. For example, the majority of male nonrated officers (55 percent) are retained through ten years, while the CCR for female nonrated officers at that point is only 37 percent. The gender differences among rated officers are even larger than among nonrated officers. Through 13 years (at which point initial service commitments would have been complete), 63 percent of male rated officers remain, on average, compared with 39 percent of female rated officers. Thus, understanding the reasons for these differences in retention rates is important for improving overall female representation within the Air Force, including among senior leaders.

Figure S.1. CCRs by Gender for Rated and Nonrated Air Force Officers

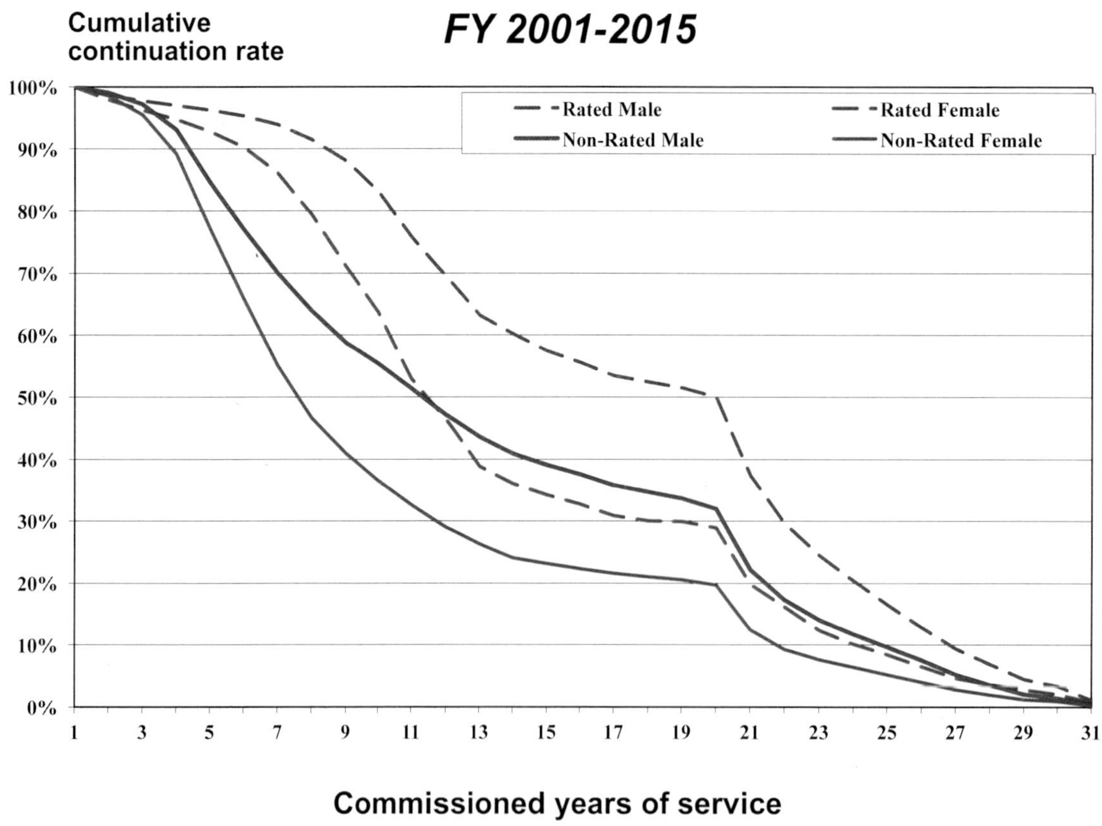

SOURCE: Air Force personnel data for August 2016 provided to RAND by the Air Force Personnel Center.

Study Objective and Methodology

The Office of the Assistant Secretary of the Air Force for Manpower and Reserve Affairs (SAF/MR) and the Air Force Deputy Chief of Staff for Manpower, Personnel and Services (AF/A1) asked RAND to conduct an exploratory qualitative study focused on gaining a better understanding of the factors that female Air Force officers consider when deciding whether to remain in or separate from the active duty Air Force and to provide recommendations for improving Air Force policies and programs to help address potential barriers and improve retention of female officers.

The Air Force already has several survey efforts focused on identifying the top personnel retention factors, and these have helped highlight gender differences in some of the top influencers (e.g., compatibility with spouse's career/job). Research also has been done examining gender differences in military career progression and retention that has highlighted the importance female service members place on such factors as marital and family status, work-family balance, occupation, aspects of the work environment, and frequency of deployments and moves when making retention decisions. However, past research has yet to be able to fully explain the gender differences in retention in the Air Force or in the U.S. armed forces more broadly (see Asch, Miller, and Weinberger, 2016; Lim et al., 2014), and further insight is still needed to better understand some of the key influencers identified through Air Force surveys.

To identify approaches that may improve retention of female Air Force officers, RAND was asked to conduct focus groups in the spring of 2016 with female officers to learn about factors that influence their decisions regarding whether to stay in or leave the active duty Air Force. Focus groups provide an opportunity to gather rich qualitative data from participants through a group discussion and are particularly useful for more-exploratory research questions, such as the focus of this study. To ensure that our focus groups were as inclusive as possible of female officers in the Air Force, we held the groups across 12 different installations that we selected based on their representation across Air Force Major Commands, various functional concentrations (e.g., intel, logistics, etc.), geographic location, and other installation characteristics (i.e., joint base, presence of a guard or reserve unit). These installations included Andrews, Barksdale, F.E. Warren, Hurlburt, Lackland, Langley, Los Angeles, McChord, Randolph, Schriever, Seymour Johnson, and Wright Patterson.

Across the 12 locations, we conducted a total of 54 focus groups that included 295 participants. The female officers who participated in the focus groups ranged in pay grade from O-1 to O-5 and represented a variety of Air Force career fields. We also included local Air Force Reserve and Air National Guard members who had previously been active duty to gather their perspectives about what factors influenced them to leave active duty. Some of our active duty focus group members had a separation date set, and we were able to get their perspectives on their decisions to leave as well. During the focus groups, which ran roughly 90 minutes in length, we asked participants about their career choices, factors that might influence a decision to stay in or leave the Air Force, and how the Air Force might improve its ability to retain female officers, in addition to general background questions.

Following completion of the focus groups, we coded transcripts from the group discussions to identify key themes common across the groups. We also coded focus group comments according to participants' background characteristics (obtained during the sessions) as a way to identify any unique trends; for example, for different pay grades or career fields. Key retention factors that emerged from the groups are described next.

Key Retention Factors for Female Air Force Officers

Through our analysis of the focus group discussion transcripts, we identified factors in four main areas that female officers in our groups highlighted as important considerations when deciding to remain in or separate from the Air Force: (1) family and personal issues, (2) career, (3) work environment, and (4) broader Air Force and military issues.

Family and Personal Factors

Family and personal life as key factors influencing retention were a prevalent theme across our focus groups with female Air Force officers. Comments included statements about children, pregnancy, spouses, dating, and other issues related to officers' personal lives. For example, all focus groups discussed children or wanting to have a family as a key retention factor, noting the difficulty of frequent moves, deployments, and demanding work schedules on children. Among the focus groups, 59 percent also noted that balancing work and family was further complicated by issues with Childcare Development Centers (CDCs), such as incompatible hours, inconsistent quality, and long waitlists. Participants in 85 percent of the groups also discussed difficulty in timing pregnancies to fit within rigid career time lines and then difficulties in finding accommodations for pumping breast milk following maternity leave (nearly half the groups discussed issues related to breastfeeding). We also asked focus groups about the importance of spouses as a retention factor, although this issue was usually raised organically by participants. Similar to concerns they expressed about children, participants cited frequent moves and deployments as challenges for both civilian and military spouses. Participants also noted that civilian male spouses often faced a lack of support from Air Force spouse groups and programs. For dual-military couples, separation due to incompatible assignments and back-to-back deployments were difficult to endure. In 48 percent of focus groups, single participants noted similar concerns regarding the negative effect of frequent moves and deployments on their relationships.

Career Factors

Beyond family and personal life factors, female officers also discussed issues related to their Air Force careers that affect their retention decisions. These career factors focused primarily on three areas: career path flexibility, ability to cross-train, and civilian opportunities. For example, 52 percent of the focus groups raised the influence of inflexibility of career paths on retention decisions. Participants described the Air Force career pyramid as a rigid career path they must follow that allows for very little deviation and few alternatives. Female officers also perceived this strict career path to often be incompatible with family and personal lives. Instead, female officers expressed the desire for alternative career paths, such as part-time options. Many participants also stated that they would prefer to continue working in the technical aspects of their career fields without transitioning to the management roles and associated demands of senior leadership. Participants in 37 percent of our focus groups also expressed a desire to cross-train into another career field, usually due to lack of interest in their current field or to find a field more compatible with a spouse also serving in the military. Finally, some female officers said they believed that opportunities in the civilian workforce might provide options more attractive than their Air Force careers in terms of pay, hours, and flexibility (raised in 43 percent of focus groups).

Work Environment Factors

Female officers also commented on several factors related to the work environment that influenced retention decisions, including the importance of leadership, female role models, mentoring, gender composition, sexual harassment and assault, and long work hours or shift work. For example, when asked about the importance of leadership on their retention decisions, participants discussed the difference that a supportive leader can have compared with a toxic one on job satisfaction, motivation, and desire to remain. In 83 percent of focus groups, the importance of having female role models in senior leadership positions was also discussed, with participants noting that they rarely see female leaders who are married with children. As a result, the perception among younger female officers is that it is not possible for women to both have a family and make senior leadership in the Air Force. Related to the importance of having role models, 56 percent of the focus groups discussed the importance of mentorship on career success and a desire to receive mentorship from successful females. When asked how, if at all, gender composition across career fields influenced retention decisions, participants had mixed responses. Many participants in male-dominated career fields reported often facing sexism and the existence of an "old boy's network." Some also associated male-dominated career fields with experiences of sexual harassment and assault. A few participants also cited cases in which either they or individuals they knew had decided to leave specifically because of a sexual assault. Finally, as already referenced in relation to difficulties managing work demands and family life, 85 percent of our focus groups raised long hours or shift work leading to burnout and work-life balance challenges.

Broader Air Force and Military Factors

Finally, focus group participants discussed several retention factors associated more broadly with an Air Force career. These are factors that may be important across gender given their presence across the military, but they were specifically raised as an issue in our focus groups. These included Air Force benefits, Permanent Change of Station (PCS), deployments, and force reduction. For example, participants in 54 percent of our focus groups raised a number of Air Force benefits that were important in deciding to remain in the service, including health care, education, and retirement benefits. In contrast to benefits as a positive influencer, nearly all focus groups discussed PCS (93 percent) and deployments (94 percent) as important negative influencers, particularly due to the effect on spouses and children. Lastly, a few participants, in 15 percent of focus groups, raised specific concerns about recent force reductions, where the Air Force cuts members to reduce manning levels, and how this created a perceived lack of job security or instability and affected their decisions to stay in.

Recently Established Air Force Programs and Policies

Focus group discussions also sought to gauge female officers' opinions about two recently established Air Force programs and policies. The first of these was the updated maternity leave policy, which extended maternity leave to 12 paid weeks and deferred fitness tests and deployments for one year after the birth of a child. The second was the Career Intermission Program (CIP), which allows for inactivation and transfer to the Individual Ready Reserve with partial pay for up to three years before returning to active duty.

Participants' comments about the updated maternity leave policy were generally positive. Female officers said the new policy is a step in the right direction to support women in the Air Force, and many felt that the previous leave of six weeks was often not adequate. Responses were mixed, however, regarding whether this new policy might influence female officers' decisions regarding retention. Some participants also expressed concern over taking a longer maternity leave and how that could have a negative impact on their careers. In addition to this change in maternity leave policy, some female officers raised the issue of extending paternity leave and adoption leave, saying such a change could serve to assist mothers with caring for newborns and could even somewhat reduce the stigma associated with only female officers taking maternity leave.

When we asked focus group participants about the CIP, understanding and awareness of the program varied. Most female officers were glad the CIP exists and thought that it could be beneficial. However, most focus group participants believed it would have little effect on retention and were skeptical that it would not have negative career effects. Some female officers also said participation in the CIP might be viewed differently by leadership and peers depending on how participants used their time away from the Air Force.

Recommendations

In Table S.1, we provide recommendations for addressing the key factors raised in the focus groups. We do not provide separate recommendations for every factor or theme mentioned within the groups; instead, we focus on recommendations that are designed to address the most-prominent themes or that may have a broad effect across several key factors. In general, these initiatives fall into three broad categories of action: (1) dissemination of additional information or education, (2) enhancements to existing programs or policies, and (3) broader structural changes to the personnel system. In several cases, the initiatives we identified are consistent with changes already proposed for the U.S. Department of Defense (DoD) by Defense Secretary Ashton Carter as part of his Force of the Future initiatives starting in 2015 (denoted by an * in the table; see DoD, 2015b; DoD, 2016a; DoD, 2016b).

Table S.1. Initiatives for Addressing Barriers to Female Officer Retention

Focus Area	Initiatives	Implementation
Family and Personal Factors		
Children	• Expand subsidized child care options and available CDC hours* • Increase paternity and adoption leave*	• Quick win • Contributor to incremental change
Breastfeeding support	• Ensure women are provided a designated nursing facility or a private room for pumping*	• Contributor to incremental change
Civilian spouse support	• Ensure spouse support programs and initiatives are inclusive of male spouses	• Contributor to incremental change
Military spouse support	• Consider a couple's parental status and needs in deployment policy • Identify an interservice liaison to coordinate cross-service spouse assignments	• Contributor to incremental change
Career Factors		
Career field knowledge	• Provide tools for educating precommissioning officers on career field options, including differences in locations, deployments, spouse compatibility, etc.	• Quick win
Cross-training	• Provide a structure and related policy for allowing more cross-training opportunities	• Quick win
Career flexibility	• Offer a separate technical career track • Expand and raise awareness of the CIP* • Provide flexibility for transferring into and back from the Air Force Reserve	• Enduring systemic change
Work Environment Factors		
Leadership and family	• Provide education for leaders on creating positive work-life balance	• Contributor to incremental change
Leadership and sexual harassment or assault	• Provide education for leaders on prevention of a sexist work environment	• Contributor to incremental change
Role modeling and mentoring	• Provide opportunities for women-focused panels or forums	• Contributor to incremental change
Broader Air Force or Military Factors		
PCS assignment process	• Explore options for reducing the frequency of PCS* • Explore a more decentralized assignment process to allow officers more autonomy in assignments	• Enduring systemic change

* Mentioned in already proposed DoD changes for developing the Force of the Future (DoD, 2015b; DoD, 2016a; DoD, 2016b).

It is important to note that the proposed initiatives in Table S.1 vary in their difficulty to implement and in their potential to significantly affect female officer retention in the Air Force. Therefore, to aid the Air Force in thinking about the best way to move forward with any proposed recommendations, we offer a suggested framework to help identify which initiatives it may want to prioritize and which initiatives may need further study prior to implementation. Specifically, we categorize each proposed initiative based on its difficulty to implement and its potential for impact on female officer retention in the Air Force. We define implementation difficulty based on the relative complexity of implementation (e.g., potential for unintended consequences due to required changes in other personnel management systems or policies). The higher the complexity to implement, likely also the higher amount of time required to do so effectively. We base the potential for impact on the number of retention factors an initiative may be able to address or the prominence of the retention factor among our focus groups.

As shown in the far right hand column of Table S.1, those initiatives that are easier to implement and have higher potential for impact could be considered *quick wins*. Those initiatives that are more difficult to implement due to required structural and policy changes but still have higher potential for impact, we view as contributing to *enduring systematic change*. Finally, those initiatives that are easier to implement but are likely to have lower impact, we consider *contributors to incremental change*. Relative to other initiatives, these contributors to incremental change are not as complex to implement, but in and of themselves they are not likely to have a sizeable impact on female officer retention due to their focus on a single or narrower issue. However, these initiatives can still play a role in improving the overall Air Force environment and support for female officers.

To gauge the validity of our initiatives and their placement in this framework, the research team consulted with four senior RAND researchers possessing a rich expertise in Air Force personnel processes and systems. The researchers were presented with our proposed initiatives and their placement in the framework. We then held discussions by phone or in-person to review the initiatives, their feasibility, and their placement within the framework. Comments from these experts were incorporated into our final recommendations.

It is important to note that the findings in this study are suggestive. They are limited in that they rely on information generated through group discussions. Therefore, the true degree to which these proposed initiatives would affect female officer retention is still unknown. Furthermore, it was beyond the scope of the current study to analyze the changes necessary for each of the proposed initiatives, especially those that would require more-complex structural and policy changes.

In addition to the initiatives proposed above, it is also important to note that military benefits (e.g., health care, education, retirement pension) were identified as one of the key positive motivators for staying in the Air Force. Therefore, changes to these benefits should be made with caution, including changes to the Basic Allowance for Housing, which was called out specifically in our focus groups. Finally, many of the proposed initiatives are also likely to benefit retention for male officers as well, given that they face some of the same challenges (although perhaps to a different degree). Thus, these initiatives may help address any unnecessary barriers for retaining talent across the Air Force, but particularly for women.

As the Air Force moves forward with making changes to improve retention of the force, and of female officers in particular, monitoring the effect of any changes will be important. This can be done through current Air Force retention surveys or follow-up focus groups or feedback panels. This will help ensure that any new initiatives are having their desired effect and help highlight continuing or new areas that may need to be addressed.

Acknowledgments

We thank Daniel R. Sitterly, Office of the Assistant Secretary of the Air Force for Manpower and Reserve Affairs (SAF/MR) and Lt Gen Gina M. Grosso and Robert E. Corsi, Air Force Deputy Chief of Staff for Manpower, Personnel and Services (AF/A1) for the opportunity to conduct this study. We also appreciate the support and guidance provided by our project monitors: Jeffrey R. Mayo (SAF/MR) and Chevalier Cleaves and Col Angela Giddings (AF/A1V). This study would not have been possible without the Airman and Family Readiness Centers that helped in coordinating the focus groups. Therefore, we are particularly grateful to Tamre Newton and Margaret Rayfield for their support of this effort. We are also thankful to Wendy Link, who went above and beyond in her assistance as we conducted our focus groups. In addition, we are indebted to the following Airman and Family Readiness Center representatives who helped with the focus group coordination and logistics: Roseline Anderson, Mark Brice-Baum, Della Gooding, Cathy Howard, Debora Jefferson, Cheryl Jensen, Kathleen Moree, Gary Sapp, Jim Snyder, Jacqualine Thomas, and Edwin White. We also had assistance from Capt Nicholas DeFranco and Maj Adrian De La Feuntes for our visit to Joint Base Lewis-McChord.

We also would like to thank several of our RAND colleagues for supporting the project. We thank Lisa Miyashiro, Molly Doyle, Sarah Weilant, and Astrid Cevallos for their help taking notes during the focus groups. We are also especially appreciative of the feedback provided by Al Robbert, Lisa Harrington, Darrell Jones, and Ray Conley on our final recommendations and the implementation framework we developed. In addition, Lt Col Kelly Sams provided helpful feedback on our recommendations and background information on relevant Air Force policies during her time in the RAND Air Force Fellows program. Finally, we appreciate the thoughtful reviews and feedback from our technical reviewers: Daniel Ginsburg, Gabriella Gonzalez, and Marek Posard. Their comments helped greatly improve the quality of this work.

Abbreviations

ADSC	Active Duty Service Commitment
AFI	Air Force Instruction
AFSC	Air Force Specialty Code
BAH	Basic Allowance for Housing
AFPC	Air Force Personnel Center
CCR	cumulative continuation rate
CDC	Childcare Development Center
CIP	Career Intermission Program
CONUS	continental United States
CYOS	commissioned year of service
DoD	U.S. Department of Defense
FY	fiscal year
MAJCOM	Air Force Major Command
OCONUS	outside continental United States
NDAA	National Defense Authorization Act
PCS	Permanent Change of Station
PME	Professional Military Education
TDY	temporary duty assignment

1. Introduction

With a focus on the potential value of diversity for improving innovation, agility, and ultimately, the mission, the U.S. armed forces has long worked toward trying to improve demographic representation within its ranks, including the representation of women (see Lucas and Segal, 2012). In the Air Force, Chief of Staff Gen David L. Goldfein has stated that, "Recruiting and retaining diverse Airmen cultivates innovation. Like different aircraft and missions make up one Air Tasking Order, different people make the best teams when integrated purposefully together" (U.S. Air Force, undated). To this end, in March 2015 and September 2016, the Air Force implemented a series of initiatives to try to improve diversity, including female representation within its ranks (see Secretary of the U.S. Air Force, 2015a; 2015b; 2016).

When it comes to improving female representation in the officer corps, military personnel statistics have shown a pattern for many years in which female officers in all services are generally less likely to progress through career milestones at the same rates as male officers. One consequence of this pattern is low female representation at the highest levels of leadership. In the Air Force in 2016, female officers made up 21.1 percent of officers in pay grades O-1 (second lieutenant) through O-5 (lieutenant colonel), but only 13.9 percent of officers at the O-6 level (colonel), and only 7.5 percent of officers at brigadier general (O-7) or higher.[4] Some of this gap represents a cohort effect—because female representation among entry cohorts has increased over time, comparing recent senior officers with cotemporaneous junior officers likely overestimates the gender difference in continuation. Still, prior work that the Air Force has sponsored on this topic has shown that female representation in each pay grade is lower than representation among the corresponding accession cohorts (Lim et al., 2014).

While there is considerable complexity in pinpointing the most effective way to improve female officer career progression and representation, prior work highlights several personnel dynamics that are of primary concern. On the promotion side, female Air Force officers tend to be concentrated in nonrated occupations (i.e., occupations in positions not related to flying),[5] which have fewer opportunities for advancement (Lim et al., 2014). Much of this difference may stem from gender differences in preferences, as prior work (e.g., Schulker, 2010) shows that women are less likely to choose rated occupations (i.e., flying-related positions, such as pilot, navigator, combat systems officer, or Air Battle Manager). In addition to these promotion-related differences, research also shows that persistent differences in retention are an important driver of

---

[4] Based on Air Force personnel data for August 2016 provided to RAND from the Air Force Personnel Center.

[5] This pattern is not unique to the Air Force. The Military Leadership Diversity Commission (2011) notes that active component officers with "tactical/operational backgrounds" tend to populate the highest levels of leadership and that these occupations tend to have higher concentrations of white male officers.

the differences in officer career progression for men and women both in the Air Force and in the military services more broadly (Asch, Miller, and Malchiodi, 2012; Hosek et al., 2001; Lim et al., 2014). However, the reasons for these gender differences in retention have yet to be fully explained (Asch, Miller, and Weinberger, 2016; Lim et al., 2014). Therefore, one of the most significant policy gaps to date is in identifying potential changes to personnel policy that can shift the number of female officers who seek to remain in service through the senior leader ranks.

Gender Differences in Air Force Officer Retention Patterns

Only 20.6 percent of officers in the Air Force are women, and, as described previously, female representation declines significantly in the higher pay grades. As one contributing factor, data show that female officers leave the Air Force at significantly higher rates earlier in their careers than do male officers. Figure 1.1 illustrates the gender differences in Air Force officer retention by showing cumulative continuation rates (CCRs) based on Air Force personnel data from fiscal year (FY) 2001 to FY 2015;[6] the CCR for each commissioned year of service (CYOS) represents the average rate of continuation through that year and all previous years.[7]

We show gender-specific retention patterns for officers in rated and nonrated occupations separately because rated occupations (and most notably, pilots) have longer initial service commitments associated with the required training.[8] And, as noted previously, prior research has found that female Air Force officers are less likely to be in rated occupations (Lim et al., 2014).[9] The figure shows that officers in rated occupations tend to have higher CCRs in general, as would be expected. Even within each set of occupations, however, female officers tend to have lower continuation rates than male officers. For example, the majority of male nonrated officers (55 percent) are retained through ten years, while the CCR for female nonrated officers at that point is only 37 percent. The gender differences among rated officers are even larger. Through 13 years (at which point most initial service commitments would be complete), 63 percent of male rated officers remain, on average, compared with 39 percent of female rated officers.

---

[6] Air Force personnel data for August 2016 was provided to RAND by the Air Force Personnel Center.

[7] To form the CCRs, we first calculate the percentage of officers in each CYOS who remained through the next CYOS. Then, we multiply these CYOS-specific continuation rates to form the CCR curves. The CCR for each CYOS, then, is the average rate of continuation through that year and all previous years. For example, the CCR for CYOS 2 is the percentage all officers who remained through their first and second year of service, while the CCR for CYOS 20 is the percentage of officers retained through 20 years of service. We were not able to separate out individuals who left due to involuntary downsizing.

[8] Most Air Force officer occupations require a four-year active duty service commitment. However, pilots make a ten-year, active duty service commitment, and both Combat System Officers and Air Battle Managers make a six-year active duty service commitment.

[9] Therefore, it is important to examine whether there are differences in retention patterns between rated and nonrated occupations—part of the aggregate retention differences could be the result of the longer service commitments for rated officers, who are more likely to be male.

Figure 1.1. Cumulative Continuation Rates by Gender for Rated and Nonrated Air Force Officers

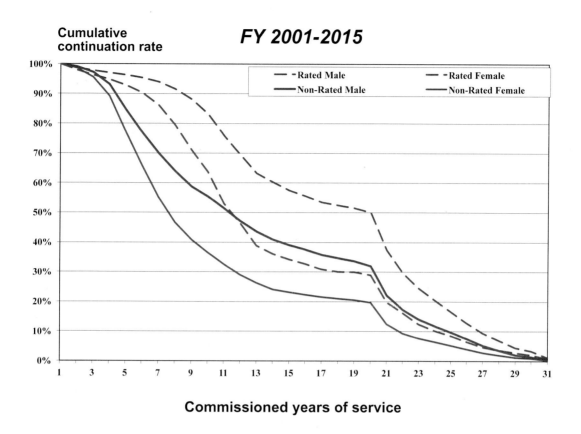

Cumulative
continuation rate

FY 2001-2015

Commissioned years of service

SOURCE: Air Force personnel data for August 2016 provided to RAND by the Air Force Personnel Center.

For both the rated and nonrated subsets of occupations, female officers require only 11 years to reach the same CCR level that male officers reach after 20 years. At the 20-year point, just under half of the rated male officers remain before retirements accelerate and the CCRs rapidly decrease. By contrast, more than half of the female rated officers are gone by CYOS 11. For nonrated male officers, 32 percent continue through CYOS 20, while female nonrated officers again cross the 32-percent threshold by CYOS 11.

Even among rated officers, there are still gender differences in occupations. Figure 1.2 shows the CCR calculations for pilots only, separating out those officers who are fighter pilots (i.e., pilots whose major weapon system is a fighter aircraft, such as an F-16, F-15, A-10, F-22). Again, female retention tends to be lower than male retention at most career points. Among male (nonfighter) pilots, 61 percent remain through 13 years, compared with 39 percent of female (nonfighter) pilots. Even among fighter pilots, female retention tends to be much lower than male retention—the rates imply that 37 percent of female fighter pilots continue through 20 years compared with 52 percent of male fighter pilots. Alternatively, female fighter pilots reach the male level of 20-year retention in CYOS 13, or seven years earlier. Given the strong relationship between experience as a fighter pilot and advancement to the senior levels (see Lim et al., 2014), this difference could represent a significant loss in human capital and a potential barrier to female representation at the highest levels of leadership.

Figure 1.2. Cumulative Continuation Rates by Gender for Fighter Pilots and Pilots of Nonfighter Major Weapon Systems

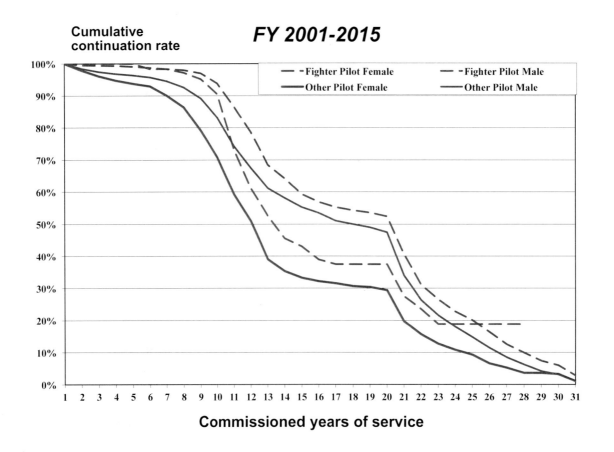

SOURCE: Air Force personnel data for August 2016 provided to RAND by the Air Force Personnel Center.

Study Objective and Approach

The Office of the Assistant Secretary of the Air Force for Manpower and Reserve Affairs (SAF/MR) and the Air Force Deputy Chief of Staff for Manpower, Personnel and Services (AF/A1) asked RAND to conduct an exploratory qualitative study focused on gaining a better understanding of the factors that female Air Force officers consider when they are deciding whether to remain in or separate from the active duty Air Force. Based on these findings, the study also aims to provide recommendations for improving Air Force policies and programs to help address potential retention barriers for female officers and improve the overall representation of female Air Force officers.

The Air Force already has several survey efforts focused on identifying the top retention factors of its personnel. This includes a Career Decisions survey administered to random samples of active duty and active guard reserve officers and enlisted personnel, excluding those who are retiring or involuntarily separating. The Air Force also has a Military Exit Survey that is offered to active duty and active guard reserve officers and enlisted personnel with an established date of separation. Results from these surveys have helped highlight top influencers for staying and leaving the Air Force, including any gender differences. For example, Air Force summaries of the results of the 2011–2012 Career Decisions survey show that the following five factors were rated as having the strongest influence on intentions to the leave the Air Force prior to serving 20 years (Air Force Personnel Center [AFPC], 2013): amount of additional duties, number of deployments, deploy-to-dwell ratio, compatibility with spouse's career or job, and opportunity to do something other than military work. When looking at these factors along gender lines, the top influencer for leaving the Air Force among female officers who intended to separate was compatibility with spouse's career or job, whereas it ranked ninth for males intending to separate. For both males and females who intended to remain in the Air Force for at least 20 years, the top reasons for staying were the retirement program, the overall compensation and benefits package, and availability of medical care.

Air Force summaries of results from the 2015 retention survey show that among those separating and those intending to separate before completing 20 years of service, maintaining work-life balance and meeting family commitments were the top influencers for leaving or intending to leave (Olson, 2016). For individuals who intended to remain in the Air Force for at least 20 years, the top reasons for staying were, again, the retirement program and the overall compensation and benefits package. When compared by gender, single female officers and single male officers shared the same sentiment toward staying, but O-1 (second lieutenant) to O-3 (captain) married female officers' intent to remain was significantly lower than that of males. Further, the surveys report that the top influences to leave cited by married female officers differed from those of their male counterparts. These influencers included compatibility with a spouse's career or job, consideration of a spouse also serving in the military (referred to as a joint spouse), children's needs, starting a family, job stress, satisfaction with current career field, and leadership at the unit level.

In addition to the Air Force's survey efforts, there has also been research examining gender differences in military career progression and retention. This research has highlighted the importance of similar retention factors as identified through the Air Force surveys, including the importance of marital and family status, work-family balance, occupation, aspects of the work environment, and frequency of deployments and moves. (See Appendix A for a more detailed review.) However, gender differences in retention in the Air Force or U.S. armed forces more broadly have yet to be fully explained (see Asch, Miller, and Weinberger, 2016; Lim et al., 2014). Further, providing greater detail and context on the ways in which already-identified factors influence female officer retention is important in helping develop more-targeted initiatives to address potential retention barriers.

Current Study

For the current qualitative effort, RAND was asked to conduct focus groups with female Air Force officers regarding the factors they consider when deciding to remain in or separate from the active duty Air Force. Focus groups provide an opportunity to gather rich qualitative data from participants through a group discussion. They are a particularly useful research method for more-exploratory research questions, such as the focus of this study. Focus groups can also help provide insight into participant perceptions and attitudes on various topics and provide an opportunity for the facilitator to clarify responses and develop a deeper understanding of issues. Also, unlike surveys, focus groups provide an opportunity for participants to explain opinions and raise new issues instead of merely responding to the limited number of choices usually presented in a survey format. Therefore, focus groups are very useful when trying to identify the most-relevant issues and can help provide additional insight and context regarding data collected through other methods. Similarly, focus groups can also help inform future data-collection efforts—for example, by identifying additional retention influencers that may be important to assess on future surveys of Air Force personnel. Finally, focus groups allow participants to comment on their own experiences in relation to topics brought up by others in the group, providing a more dynamic discussion of different perspectives.

For the current study, focus groups allowed us to see if participants would raise similar or different issues than had been identified through previous research and Air Force surveys. The groups also provided an opportunity to gather more information surrounding these issues (e.g., what aspects of the work environment are important influencers of retention, or in what specific ways a spouse's career or children's needs influence retention decisions). In addition, this approach allowed us to ask participants about their own thoughts regarding what changes to Air Force policies and programs might help improve retention of female officers. At the request of the study sponsors, we also included questions focused on recent changes in the maternity leave policy and the Career Intermission Program (CIP). In early 2016, the Air Force extended maternity leave from six continuous, fully paid weeks to 12, in compliance with new Department of Defense (DoD)–wide policy changes (Air Force Instruction [AFI] 36-3003). Under the new policy, women can also defer fitness tests and deployments for one year after the birth of a child. At the time of this study, the CIP was a pilot program that allowed for inactivation and transfer to the Individual Ready Reserve with partial pay for up to three years before returning to active duty.[10]

---

[10] The 2009 National Defense Authorization Act (NDAA) provided initial authorization for the services to implement career intermission pilot programs, with the 2015 NDAA then extending the service authority to conduct these programs through calendar year 2019 (Pub. L. 110-417, 2008; Pub. L. 113-219, 2014). The Air Force implemented these pilot programs in 2014 (U.S. Government Accountability Office, 2015).

To ensure that our focus groups were as inclusive of female officers in the Air Force as possible, we held the groups across 12 different installations that we selected based on their representation across Air Force Major Commands (MAJCOMs), various functional concentrations (e.g., intel, logistics, etc.), and other installation characteristics. We provide greater detail on our methodology in Chapter 2.

Based on our focus group findings, we identify potential initiatives that the Air Force could take to help address key retention factors. To aid the Air Force in thinking about how to prioritize any of the proposed recommendations, we also place these initiatives in a broader framework based on their difficulty to implement and their potential for impact on female officer retention in the Air Force. To gauge the validity of the initiatives assessed in this framework, the research team also consulted with four senior RAND researchers possessing a rich expertise in Air Force personnel processes and systems. The researchers were presented with our proposed initiatives and their placement in the framework. We then held discussions by phone or in person to review the initiatives, their feasibility, and their placement within the framework. Comments from these experts were incorporated into our final recommendations.

Limitations

It is important to note that there are several limitations to this study. First, although there are considerable benefits to taking a qualitative approach through the use of focus groups, focus groups provide purely descriptive information. When describing our findings in the report, we provide the percentage of groups in which a particular topic or issue was raised to help provide a general sense of a how often a theme was discussed. However, focus groups involve the use of open-ended questions in which different groups may raise and discuss different issues and not all members of a focus group comment on every question. Therefore, we are not able to provide statistical estimates regarding the relative importance of any single factor or the percentage of individual participants for which a particular factor is important in retention decisions. Instead, these results are intended to be descriptive and provide greater insight and context on retention issues. In addition, although we attempted to sample participants from across the Air Force by targeting installations based on their representation of different key characteristics, we still have a relatively small sample compared with the overall Air Force population, and we do not know the extent to which participant views are generalizable to the larger population of female Air Force officers. This is expected with focus groups, but it is still important to note when interpreting the findings. Finally, it was beyond the scope of this study to hold similar groups for male officers and see if we heard similar or different factors and suggestions for improvements. Acknowledging these limitations, the focus groups in this report were able to provide rich context and insight into key retention factors for Air Force female officers, including potential policy and program changes that the Air Force can further explore to address barriers.

Organization of the Report

The remaining chapters in this report document the study findings and recommendations. Chapter 2 provides an overview of our focus group methodology, including the participants, focus group structure, and coding and analysis processes. Chapter 3 describes the key retention factors identified through the focus groups. Finally, Chapter 4 presents our overall conclusions and recommendations for improving Air Force policies and programs to help address potential barriers and improve female officer retention. The report also includes four appendixes. Appendix A presents a high-level overview of relevant prior research on retention differences between women and men in both the military and civilian worlds. Appendix B provides greater detail on the selection of Air Force bases for conducting the focus groups. Appendixes C and D present the focus group protocols and additional details on our approach for coding the data.

2. Focus Group Methodology

To identify approaches that might improve retention of female Air Force officers, we conducted focus groups with female officers in the spring of 2016 to learn about factors that influence their decisions regarding whether to stay in or separate from the active duty Air Force. To ensure that our focus groups were as inclusive as possible of female officers in the Air Force, we held the groups across 12 different continental United States installations selected to provide representation across MAJCOMs, various functional concentrations (e.g., intel, logistics, pilots, etc.), geographic locations, and other installation characteristics (i.e., joint base status and presence of a local guard or reserve unit). These locations included Andrews, Barksdale, F.E. Warren, Hurlburt, Lackland, Langley, Los Angeles, McChord, Randolph, Schriever, Seymour Johnson, and Wright Patterson (Figure 2.1). Appendix B provides greater detail regarding our base selection methodology.

Figure 2.1. Air Force Bases Included in Focus Group Sample

Participants

Our team worked with the Airmen and Family Readiness Centers at each location to connect with potential focus group participants. Representatives from the Airmen and Family Readiness Centers emailed all active duty female officers at their locations who had up to 12 years of service, asking for volunteers to participate in the RAND focus groups. In consultation with the study sponsors, we chose to target female officers specifically in this year range because the majority of attrition for female officers happens earlier in their careers. We went out to 12 years to account for the longer initial service commitment required by certain rated specialties. Some of our focus group members had a separation date set, so we were also able to get their perspectives on their decisions to leave.

Across the 12 locations, we conducted a total of 54 focus groups that included 295 participants. The female officers who participated in the focus groups ranged in pay grade from O-1 to O-5. The breakdown of participants by pay grade and comparison to pay grade distribution across total female officers in the Air Force is detailed in Table 2.1.[11]

Table 2.1. Focus Group Participants by Pay Grade

Pay Grade	Focus Group Sample (#)	Focus Group Sample (%)	Air Force Females	O-1 to O-5 Air Force Females (%)
O-1	45	15%	1,514	13%
O-2	42	14%	1,686	14%
O-3	135	46%	4,838	40%
O-4	64	22%	2,532	21%
O-5	7	2%	1,468	12%
Missing	2	1%	NA	NA

SOURCE: AFPC, Interactive Demographic Analysis System [IDEAS], officer extract data, August 2016.
NOTE: Percentages may not equal 100 due to rounding.

Focus group participants represented a variety of Air Force career fields. Table 2.2 details participants' career field breakdown and a comparison to the distribution of career field groups for all Air Force female officers.[12]

---

[11] We do not have information on overall participation rates as RAND did not have information on the number of individuals who received invitations for participation. We do know that the invite was sent to all female officers at each base with up to 12 years of service. To ensure we did not have a biased sample, we compared the backgrounds of participants in our groups with the general Air Force population as shown in Tables 2.1–2.3.

[12] Operations = Pilot, Navigator, Combat Systems Officer, Air Battle Manager, Combat Rescue/Special Tactics, Space, Missiles, Intel, Cyber, Remotely Piloted Aircraft; Logistics = Maintenance, Logistics; Support = Security Forces, Civil Engineer, Public Affairs, Personnel, Support; Medical = Doctors, Dentists, Nurses, Social Workers, Flight Surgeons; Professional = Judge Advocate General, Chaplain; Acquisitions = Scientists, Engineers (except Civil), Contracting, Finance, Acquisition. We did not have pay grade information for two participants. Participants were allowed to pass or omit any information they do not want to share.

Table 2.2. Focus Group Participants by Career Field Group

Career Field	Focus Group Sample (#)	Focus Group Sample (%)	Air Force Females	O-1 to O-5 Air Force Females (%)
Operations	87	30%	3,013	25%
Logistics	23	8%	616	5%
Support	46	16%	900	8%
Medical	63	21%	4,648	39%
Professional	19	6%	400	3%
Acquisitions	54	18%	990	8%
Special investigation	2	1%	101	1%
Special duty	1	<1%	290	2%

SOURCE: AFPC, IDEAS, officer extract data, August 2016.
NOTE: Percentages may not equal 100 due to rounding or due to "ERROR" values, and the exclusion of reporting identifiers for AFPC data. Our protocol asked respondents "What is your career field" to determine officers' Air Force Specialty Codes (AFSCs) and did not specify between primary and duty specialties. An officer's primary AFSC is that specialty in which she has the highest skill level, while her duty AFSC is that of the position she currently occupies. While these occasionally differ, these differences were determined to be minimal. The comparison case of O-1–O-5 Air Force female AFSC distributions is based on duty AFSC data drawn from AFPC.

We also asked focus group participants to share their commissioning source. Table 2.3 outlines this information and the total Air Force female officer comparison.[13]

Table 2.3. Focus Group Participants by Commissioning Source

Commissioning Source	Focus Group Sample (#)	Focus Group Sample (%)	Air Force Females	O-1 to O-5 Air Force Females (%)
U.S. Air Force Academy	60	20%	2,010	17%
Reserve Officer Training Corps	130	44%	4,339	36%
Officer Training School	35	12%	1,602	13%
Direct	62	21%	3,888	32%
Missing	8	3%	NA	NA

SOURCE: AFPC, IDEAS, officer extract data, August 2016.
NOTE: Focus group percentages may not equal 100 due to rounding or due to the exclusion of "Other" and "Air Force National Guard" commissions from AFPC data.

We also wanted to include perspectives of prior active duty Reserve Component and Air National Guard female officers where possible to learn about factors that influenced these

---

[13] We did not have commissioning source information on eight participants. Participants were allowed to pass or omit any information they do not want to share.

officers to leave the active duty Air Force. When coordinating focus group visits with Airmen and Family Readiness Center representatives, we requested that they reach out to leadership of local Air Force Reserve and Air National Guard units to solicit volunteers for focus groups. For locations where representatives were able to connect with local Reserve or Guard units, responses were limited. This was often due to scheduling difficulties related to coordination with civilian jobs, because focus groups were held during the day, and/or proximity to the base. For the Reserve Component officers who did participate, some were in focus groups composed exclusively of Reserve Component officers, while some were mixed in with groups of active duty officers. In total, 14 Reserve Component officers participated in the focus groups. Their responses regarding the factors that led them to leave active duty were consistent with the themes we heard from current active duty members.

Focus Group Structure

Focus groups began by providing participants with background information about the study and administering informed consent. This included emphasizing the voluntary nature of participation and assuring participants that any individually identifying information they provided would be kept confidential by the research team. The focus groups ran roughly 90 minutes in length, during which time participants were asked about their career choices, factors that could influence whether they decide to stay in or leave the Air Force, and how the Air Force might improve its ability to retain female officers, in addition to general background questions. Appendix C provides the full focus group protocols. Each session was facilitated by one RAND team member with a second team member taking notes. Facilitators and note takers were both female researchers to ensure the comfort of the participants when discussing their experiences as women in the Air Force. Note takers did not include names or other identifiable information about the participants in the notes. Additionally, focus group participants were given the opportunity to provide written comments to the research team at the end of the session if there were comments they wanted to share but did not feel comfortable voicing in front of the group. We added these comments to the session's notes.

Qualitative Coding and Analysis

Once we completed all focus groups, we uploaded the detailed focus group transcripts into NVivo, a qualitative data analysis software program. RAND researchers coded written transcripts from the focus groups to identify key themes common across the groups. We used an integrated approach of deductive and inductive coding, with the protocol questions guiding the initial development of codes. We then incorporated additional themes that emerged within these broader codes throughout the coding process. We also coded focus group comments according to participants' background characteristics (obtained during the sessions) so we could identify any unique trends; for example, for different pay grades or career fields. The coding was divided

12

between two research team members, and we ensured that we had sufficient interrater reliability by calculating Cohen's kappa.[14] Appendix D provides a more detailed overview of our approach to content coding and interrater reliability, along with the coding guides. Chapter 3 describes the key retention factors identified from our focus groups.

---

[14] Cohen's Kappa coefficient (Cohen, 1960) is a statistical measure of interrater reliability that aims to account for coding agreement occurring by chance. Guidelines recommended for interpreting Kappa values are as follows: below 0.40—poor agreement, 0.40–0.75—fair to good agreement, above 0.75—excellent agreement.

3. Key Retention Factors for Female Air Force Officers

In this chapter, we describe the key themes that emerged from our focus groups with female Air Force officers regarding factors they consider when deciding to stay in or separate from the active duty Air Force. Overall, female officers identified retention factors that fell into four main areas (1) family and personal issues, (2) career, (3) work environment, and (4) broader Air Force and military-related issues. We discuss the more-specific concerns and considerations identified within each of these broader categories in the sections that follow. We also asked focus group participants to provide feedback on two recently established Air Force policies and programs: the updated maternity leave policy and the CIP. Where relevant, we note any differences we heard across career fields or differences between single and married officers.[15]

Family and Personal Factors

When asked what factors in general contributed to female officers leaving the Air Force, almost all focus groups voluntarily raised the importance of family or other personal matters. We then specifically asked participants to discuss the ways in which personal matters or family may influence their retention decisions. Comments within this theme include statements about children, pregnancy, breastfeeding, spouses, dating, and other issues related to officers' personal lives. Every focus group discussed these issues, with participants in 74 percent of groups volunteering that family or personal factors were their top influencers regarding whether they choose to remain in the Air Force.

Some of the comments made did not identify specific components of family or personal lives, but rather discussed this topic in generic terms. For example, 88 percent of groups made general comments that family or personal lives were a key influencer in their retention decisions. For example, one participant stated,

> It's up to each individual to have their own priorities. In my experience,
> generally, men put career before family, but for me, my family is before my
> career, so if I get to the point where the Air Force is negatively affecting my
> family, I am leaving.

Many of these comments focused on issues related to difficulties managing a desired work-life balance due to the nature of an Air Force career. Also mentioned were difficulties with separation from family and the family's ability to cope with separation that resulted from deployments, joint-spouse assignment separation, or other reasons. Female officers also

---

[15] We also examined the data by pay grade and status as a Reserve or Guard member compared with active duty, but did not identify any relevant differences.

expressed that they felt the need to choose between their families and their Air Force careers and that having both was not a maintainable or feasible option over the long term.

Consistent with this finding, 2015 Air Force survey results also indicated that work-life balance and meeting family commitments were top influencers for leaving or intending to leave the Air Force (Olson, 2016). Similar concerns regarding family and work-life balance for women in the military have been raised in other studies as well, with scholars asserting that although the conflict also exists for men, it is generally greater for women (e.g., Coser, 1974; Segal, 1986; Bourg and Segal, 1999; Hosek et al., 2001).

Next, we discuss more-specific aspects of family and personal lives that affect female officer retention decisions.

Children

If not raised organically, which it almost always was, we asked participants specifically about how children may affect female officers' decisions regarding whether to stay in or leave the Air Force. While most of the comments we heard were from mothers, many women who did not have children also raised concerns about having children in the future while in the Air Force.

One issue that focus group participants raised was the effect of frequent moves on children. These moves can result in a lack of stability for children of Air Force officers and the loss of family support networks. Participants noted the difficulty and stress for children who must continually change schools with moves and be forced to make new friends in each new location. Moves can also result in children being separated from one parent if a joint military couple is not colocated, a civilian spouse stays behind to continue current employment, or a child stays behind with one parent to finish high school or another type of milestone. However, a small number of participants did note the positive aspects of these moves for children, mentioning that frequent moves contributed to the resiliency of their children.

Female officers also discussed the effect of deployments related to children and how this could influence their retention decisions. Participants noted the difficulties associated with leaving children for deployments and being away for important milestones in their children's lives. Comments included feelings of guilt for leaving children for an extended period of time and the fear of young children not remembering them when returning. Some participants acknowledged that this could also be an issue for male officers who are fathers. However, some commented that these types of separation issues are more pronounced for mothers. For example, one participant stated,

> I have a 2-year-old. I was previously volunteering for deployment, but if I had 365 now, and had to miss an entire year—I would get out.

Participants also noted that child care during deployments was more difficult because these responsibilities are now relegated to one parent—or perhaps other family members if both parents are deployed in a joint military couple or the female officer is a single parent. These types of separation concerns can even delay the decision to have children for some women. As one participant noted,

> The officer in me enjoys deployments and I feel effective, but thinking about the kids, and now I'm considering when we have kids. It's double edged—I don't mind deploying, but on the other side, I don't want to be away from my family or kids for an extended amount of time.

When discussing issues regarding children and retention, female officers also commented on the effect that rigid work schedules and long work hours have on their ability to spend time with their children. Schedules tend to have set hours that do not allow much flexibility for accommodating time with family. Participants also noted that many leaders expect long hours in the office, along with additional duties, that do not leave much time to be with their children.

Female officers also expressed frustration regarding child care options provided by the Air Force and emphasized how this contributes to difficulties regarding work-life balance. Participants in 59 percent of focus groups specifically raised issues related to Childcare Development Centers (CDCs). One concern that was raised focused on CDC hours being inconsistent with expected work hours and schedules—CDCs often have limited hours that make it difficult to coordinate child care with the long work hours or shift work that can be a regular part of officers' jobs. For example, one participant stated,

> I am a shift worker. Child care is so hard for a shift worker. The CDC offers 12 hours of child care, so if you work 12-hour shifts, you're really working 13 hours minimum per shift when you take into account changing clothes and finishing paperwork—and if you are a single mom or have a husband who is also a shift worker or a civilian, your only real option is to get child care on the outside.

This issue can be particularly problematic for certain career fields. For example, pilots may be required to fly at night and regularly need overnight child care, outside of typical CDC hours. Participants also expressed frustration with strict CDC policies related to pick-up times, and female officers relayed experiences of being charged by the minute for additional care if running a few minutes late coming from work to pick up children. Discussion about CDCs also focused on problems with wait lists to get access to child care: Some participants cited problems setting up child care with CDCs before the end of their maternity leaves due to lengthy wait lists.

Some female officers also raised concerns about the quality of care at CDCs. Participants noted that the quality of CDC employees is not consistent across locations and that CDCs generally do not provide day-care services that include educational activities to enhance children's learning, unlike some off-base options. Despite these concerns and frustrations with CDCs, a few participants did acknowledge that child care through a CDC is much more affordable than most off-base options. While a few participants mentioned subsidy programs for off-base child care, they also noted that these programs were not well known or understood.

Beyond concerns about CDCs, participants discussed the use of the family care plan as another issue related to child care that could affect retention decisions. Participants expressed frustration regarding leadership's confusion about how the family care plan is intended to be used. They stressed that the family care plan is to be used in emergency situations and that it should not and sometimes cannot be activated for such situations as staying late at work. For example, one participant stated,

> If you have people that don't have kids or don't think about it, they don't understand the purpose of it [the family care plan]. That family care plan is if we go to war! Not for, "I have to stay at work long one day." My mother will come and it will take her six hours to get here. So more education for supervisors about the family care plan—it can't be activated just like that.

Female officers also mentioned that they sometimes struggle to establish a family care plan within the time frame required by the Air Force when moving to a new location. This problem is predominantly an issue for joint-spouse couples or single parents, who do not have a civilian parent to serve as caretaker in their absence as part of the family care plan. When moving to a new area, it can take time to establish relationships with civilians in the area whom officers can trust to care for their children if the family care plan is activated.

Pregnancy

Issues related to pregnancy that could affect female officers' decisions whether to stay in or leave the Air Force arose in 85 percent of focus groups. One pregnancy-related concern that participants raised focused on difficulty in timing pregnancies to fit within rigid career time lines. Female officers relayed that they have felt the need to "program" pregnancy at precise times in their careers to minimize negative career effects. Despite attempts to time pregnancies, negative effects reportedly still persist due to missed opportunities while pregnant, such as in-residence Professional Military Education (PME), or career field–specific problems, such as loss of flying time for pilots. For example, one participant stated,

> If you really look into it, women officers are programming their pregnancies. I literally had an app on my phone that said when it was best to make a baby, and not just because I'm an OCD planner, but I want the baby to be happy and healthy. I fly a C-130 where there are more limitations—I can't fly when pregnant, and there are some planes you can fly in your middle trimester but not this one. I can't fly at all if I'm pregnant. But programming a pregnancy is serious stuff.

A few female officers also noted that they did not feel comfortable mentioning potential pregnancies as part of career planning discussions with their leadership.

Twenty-eight percent of focus groups raised the issue of facing pregnancy discrimination in the Air Force. Participants relayed experiences of perceived pregnancy discrimination, including moving one pregnant female officer out of a leadership position because she was told she would miss too much work, and another not receiving a career-enhancing assignment when the issue of having children came up in the interview for the position. As mentioned previously, female officers also noted being restricted to PME by correspondence while pregnant, which they stated is viewed negatively by promotion boards. In addition, participants discussed a perceived stigma associated with pregnancy in the Air Force. They described a perception by leadership and peers that female officers get pregnant to avoid deployments and that pregnant female officers are not pulling their weight and others will have to pick up the slack of their workload when they are on maternity leave.

Beyond these concerns about so-called "textbook" pregnancies, a few female officers noted a lack of Air Force support for difficulties related to pregnancy. For instance, participants in a few groups relayed negative experiences after suffering miscarriages. These female officers noted a lack of emotional support and necessary time away from work after a miscarriage and a lack of understanding from leadership. Some participants mentioned a similar lack of support and understanding from leadership related to postpartum depression. Other female officers relayed personal experiences or those of peers with the difficulties of infertility while in the Air Force. Participants noted that TRICARE coverage for many of these treatments is extremely limited. Beyond cost, some remote Air Force installations are not located near reputable fertility clinics, meaning that access to services can be limited. For female officers who do undergo infertility treatment, they noted that there are further complications for their careers. For example, necessary frequent medical appointments are difficult to balance with a rigid work schedule and reported lack of support and understanding from leadership. Career effects are also exacerbated for certain fields. For instance, a participant who is a pilot noted that pilots cannot be on flight status while on certain fertility medications. This means not only a loss of flight time that can hurt officers' records, but also a lack of privacy for the female officer because this status can make her personal issues known to peers. Additionally, a few participants mentioned that infertility decreases a female officer's ability to "program" a pregnancy at a precise time to minimize the negative effects on her career, and she can face increased stigma if the timing of her pregnancy is perceived as problematic.

Breastfeeding

Many female officers noted frustration with continuing breastfeeding when returning to work from maternity leave; 46 percent of focus groups discussed these concerns. Current Air Force policy states that "The AFMS [Air Force Medical Service] recommends that supervisors of AF members who are breastfeeding work with the member to arrange their work schedules to allow 15–30 minutes every 3–4 hours to pump breast milk in a room or an area that provides adequate privacy and cleanliness. Restrooms should not be considered an appropriate location for pumping" (AFI 44-102). However, one of the most prevalent concerns raised in our groups focused on accommodation issues related to breastfeeding. Participants reported a lack of acceptable pumping facilities at work, which made breastfeeding after returning from maternity leave difficult. Some female officers relayed experiences of having to pump in bathrooms and closets rather than in more appropriate facilities. One participant commented,

> We had a training schedule and I'd have to tell my students that I had to stop and
> pump and then walk to the next facility to do it. I had to pump in the closet.

18

Breastfeeding accommodation concerns focused not only on providing reasonable facilities but also on leadership's understanding and accommodating the time needed for pumping during the work day.

Another concern mentioned by participants was complications with breastfeeding while being sent on a temporary duty assignment (TDY) soon after returning from maternity leave. A few participants noted a lack of support for shipping breast milk home. Some relayed experiences with struggling to coordinate the logistics of shipping breast milk without Air Force support, and others noted that some female officers felt the need to stop breastfeeding their child because of the lack of support to continue when TDY.

Spouses

We asked all focus groups how spouses or partners might influence their retention decisions, but in most cases, participants raised the issue of spousal influence organically. And, in nearly all groups, participants indicated that spouses or partners were a primary influence on their career decisions. Additionally, participants in 54 percent of the groups volunteered that their spouses are the factor that has the most influence on their retention decisions. Consistent with this finding, results from the 2011–2012 Air Force surveys indicated that compatibility with a spouse's career/job was the top influencer for leaving the Air Force among females who intended to separate, among females who were married, and among single females (AFPC, 2013). Current personnel statistics indicate that 58 percent of female officers are married, 33 percent are single, and 8 percent are divorced.[16]

Issues related to spouses varied depending on whether female officers were married to civilian or military spouses, as we will now discuss in more detail.

Civilian Spouses

Almost all groups discussed issues related to civilian spouses and retention. One of the most prevalent issues that participants mentioned was the effect of frequent moves on civilian spouses' careers. Civilian spouses often have difficulty transferring jobs or finding new employment with each PCS-related move. Some noted that civilian spouses can have licensing issues with moves across state lines and that many must continually start at the bottom and work their way up at each new job. As a result, many female officers feel as though their civilian spouses' careers suffer because of the demands of the Air Force. For example, one participant commented,

> I'm on the fence about staying in. I like what I do, but I'm nervous about my husband's happiness because he is a civilian, he's a teacher, and has had a hard time finding employment. Prospective employers see on his resume how much he's moved around and are reluctant to hire him.

---

[16] Based on Air Force Personnel Data as of March 2017 provided to RAND by the Air Force Personnel Center.

In addition to the frequency of moves, some participants mentioned that the locations of some Air Force bases can be restrictive for their spouses' careers. Some locations that female officers are assigned to may lack opportunities for certain civilian careers, for example, if those careers are linked to certain regions of the country or to more metropolitan areas. As one participant noted,

> My husband is a civilian and he has to take a complete backseat . . . and he said, "I'll make that sacrifice." . . . He has a college degree and it's in forestry and he can only do that in forests! So, it's a very limited area, and he had to get a job at a high school and then at Lowes or Home Depot.

Some participants also expressed that they did not feel the Air Force assignment process took civilian spouse careers into account, such as for location preferences, when making assignment decisions. Some female officers live separately from their civilian spouses for a period of time so that civilian spouses can maintain careers. A few participants also noted that difficulties related to frequent moves and civilian spouse careers can end in divorce.

Female officers also discussed issues related to deployments and the effects they can have on marriages to civilians. Participants mentioned concerns about leaving the civilian spouse as a single parent with little support network. Separation from civilian spouses during deployments was also noted as an issue, with a few participants again suggesting that these separations can sometimes lead to divorce.

Additionally, female officers married to male civilians said their spouses often struggle with gender stereotypes in the military spouse role. Some male spouses have difficulty "following" their spouse's Air Force career from installation to installation. Participants also mentioned that male spouses of female officers, and particularly those who are stay-at-home dads, often face a stigma associated with these so-called emasculating roles.

Of the focus groups who discussed civilian spouse issues, 13 percent also discussed the lack of support for male spouses. For example, one participant stated,

> I think the military is really hard on my husband. He had started his career when I went active duty, so he had to leave his job to be with me. I've been in for five years, and he's never been contacted by spousal support and never gets it; it's all for military wives. At our last duty station, there was only one other husband who was a civilian. Here, we're the only one. He's only been able to pick up part-time jobs, so he's going to be a stay-at-home dad. What I've gotten from people is, "How do you allow your husband not to have a career?"

Participants relayed experiences with Air Force spouse groups not being inclusive of male spouses, with some explicitly stating they have an exclusively female membership. Some female officers with male civilian spouses also noted a lack of support for their spouses from the Air Force community, which is particularly difficult during deployments.

Military Spouses

Nearly all focus groups discussed issues related to military spouses and how these influence decisions on whether to stay in or leave the Air Force. Participants in 37 percent of groups volunteered that military spouse concerns were the biggest factor affecting their retention decisions. Participants noted that joint-spouse issues are more prevalent for females than males in the Air Force because more female officers are joint spouses than male officers. Data support this assertion, as Air Force personnel files show that 37 percent of married female Air Force officers are joint spouses (including cross-service joint spouses), compared with only 7 percent of married male Air Force officers.[17] The importance of joint-spouse issues has similarly been reflected in prior research on female retention in the military (e.g., Hosek et al., 2001).

One of the most frequently mentioned issues was joint-spouse separate assignments and struggles obtaining colocated assignments. Participants relayed experiences with frequent or lengthy separations or fears that they may face separation from their military spouse in the future. A few female officers had assignments that they reported were considered colocated but were actually several hours apart by car. Some participants noted feeling misled by the Air Force and had expected consistent joint assignments if married to another Air Force officer. Many also expressed a perception of a general lack of support and flexibility for joint couples in the assignment process. A few female officers reported that attempts to select compatible career fields as a means to remain located with their spouse had not paid off. For example, one participant stated,

> My junior year at academy I put in my preferences. I was engaged to a pilot at the time so my mentor suggested Intel would be a good AFSC to be stationed with a pilot husband. I went to Intel school, which happened to be located at any base except where he was (as a pilot instructor). We've been married for five years but didn't get to be in the same place until last July.

Participants noted the increased expenses related to separate assignments, including maintaining two households, leave time, and travel costs for visiting spouses, although they do receive a small monthly family separation allowance. For female officers in joint marriages who also have children, these types of separations can result in children being separated from one parent. Some female officers reported that separate assignments can also delay joint couples from starting a family. One participant commented,

> We are a joint-spouse couple, which makes it difficult. . . . We haven't lived together in two years. We've been married for eight years and lived together for 3.5 years. We would have liked to start a family but couldn't because of the separation. We decided to reevaluate things when we both hit the Major level. I

---

[17] Based on Air Force personnel data for August 2016 provided to RAND by the Air Force Personnel Center. For married female officers, 34 percent are married to active duty Air Force, and 3 percent are married to an active duty member in another service; for married male officers, 6 percent are married to active duty Air Force, and fewer than 1 percent are married to an active duty member in another service.

got picked up for school. We are on the brink of not being able to take the separation anymore.

Another issue raised was that in joint marriages, one spouse's military career must take the lead and one must take the back seat. Participants felt that the spouse whose military career generally suffered was the female rather than the male officer. For example, one participant stated,

> Joint spouse is not easy to do if you both want a career—and we were both doing well, but this assignment, I took what was last on my list, which was detrimental to me to be in the same place but I did it to stay and keep my family together. But my career has taken a nosedive because of that choice.

Deployments can also raise additional complications for female officers with military spouses. For joint couples with children, there is a fear of both spouses deploying at the same time, leaving children without a parent during this time and necessitating long-term child care plans. While staggered deployments allow for one parent in joint couples to be available to children, it can mean joint spouses with back-to-back staggered deployments have lengthy periods of separation. Female officers with military spouses without children noted that they would prefer to deploy at the same time as their spouses to avoid additional prolonged separation.

A few participants mentioned that joint-spouse issues are exacerbated in certain career fields. For example, career fields that have very limited location assignment options or those with high operational tempos can be more difficult to manage. Separation or child care concerns can be more prevalent in these types of career fields. Specifically, pilots were identified as a career that can cause additional complications for joint spouses.

When asked about issues related to having a military spouse, several female officers raised a concern about the potential removal of the Basic Allowance for Housing (BAH) for one member of a joint couple. For military members who are married to another military member, both spouses are eligible to receive a BAH. At the time of this study, the removal of BAH for one member of a dual-military couple had been proposed as part of the National Defense Authorization Act, but the legislation was not yet approved. Ultimately, the proposal was dropped from the final version of the policy bill. Participants expressed that they felt this removal of BAH would be unfair, would likely affect females to a greater extent than males, and would be reason enough they would consider leaving the Air Force.

Dating

According to Air Force personnel statistics, roughly 33 percent of female officers are unmarried or single.[18] For single female officers, dating was an important issue, with nearly half of the focus groups (48 percent) discussing issues related to dating as a factor affecting their retention decisions. Participants noted that it is difficult for female officers in the Air Force to

---

[18] Based on Air Force Personnel Data as of March 2017 provided to RAND by the Air Force Personnel Center.

maintain dating relationships because of the instability related to frequent PCS moves and deployments. For example, one participant stated,

> I'm supposed to PCS next summer and I'm seeing someone now, and do I stop seeing someone or a few months before [moving], I just don't date? I'm only 27 now but how many more times in the last few months of an assignment will this happen because I'm going to move—is it worth it to keep going with the relationship? Because part of the reason to stay [in the Air Force] is I don't have passion for civilian work—if I did, I'd probably be out already. . . . I enjoy what I do, and there's nothing out there that's sparkly to drive me out, and I'm good at what I do. But those factors . . . and I come back from deployment and I only come home to a dog and I want to come home to a partner.

Participants noted that difficulties maintaining dating relationships are often harder for female officers than for male officers, if in heterosexual relationships, as societal norms make men less likely to be willing to follow a woman for her career, as mentioned earlier regarding civilian spouse issues. Thus, relationships for female officers often come to a crossroads with each move. For female officers dating other Airmen, they described decisions about marriage being forced on couples very early in a relationship in order to seek colocation and continue the relationship. Like many married female officers, single female officers felt they often needed to choose between their career and their relationship and faced issues similar to married women regarding separation.

Another issue that participants mentioned was the effect of Air Force base locations on dating. Some bases are located in remote areas and do not have large populations of civilian single young professionals that female officers would seek as a dating pool. For example, one participant stated,

> The Air Force is restricting for dating options. I'm single and in my thirties and those [people] usually live in cities, and there are only four bases in cities. I want to go where other single professionals are.

Single female officers noted that an Air Force career can delay marriage and children because frequent moves, deployments, location, and the lack of work-life balance result in limited opportunities for dating. Single females expressed that they can often feel "invisible" in the Air Force, with most programs focused on supporting families. They feel they are often tapped for extra hours in the office and additional deployments because of their single status. A few participants noted that there is sometimes a stigma that exists for female officers who are single and dating that does not similarly exist for male officers. One participant commented,

> It's hard for female officers. You have no one to talk to. . . . For officers, and especially for single female officers, it's tough to find fellow single officers that can understand the things you're going through, who don't have children, know how to relate. . . . You are criticized for living a single life. As an officer, you should not be going to bars. I was told, "Lieutenant, stay in your house, close your blinds and drink wine." I said I joined a dating site and my leadership said "Lieutenant, you shouldn't do that. You have to be careful."

Additional Family and Personal Factors

In addition to the family and personal factors already described, female officers raised a few other issues related to family and personal lives, but with less frequency. These included concerns about female-related health care. A few participants reported that they felt Air Force obstetric and gynecologic care was focused on pregnancy and delivering babies and lacked expertise in other gynecological specialties. Some female officers also complained that the Air Force medical system does not allow for seeing the same gynecologist for repeat visits, which they noted could be an issue for chronic or undiagnosed female health issues. A few participants mentioned that they would like direct access to a female health appointment with a female physician without sometimes having to go through an appointment with a male physician first. In terms of pregnancy, some female officers expressed frustration with the lack of options for where they can give birth. Participants noted that in order to be covered by TRICARE, they could not have a home birth with a midwife or choose to go off-base to a civilian hospital or birthing center unless a local military treatment facility was unavailable, which they felt to be limiting.

Beyond female health care issues, another family-related factor that participants mentioned was elder care or caring for a sick parent. Female officers noted that being caregivers for aging or sick parents often falls to the women in the family and can be an added stress that is complicated by Air Force career demands. Additionally, some participants reported that it can be more difficult to establish friendships as a female in the Air Force. Because of frequent moves and resulting limited connection with the local community, officers often turn to peers at work for friendship and as a support network. However, female officers noted that this is more difficult when most of their peers are male. They sometimes worry about the perception of spending time outside work with male peers and this can also result in tensions with male peers' civilian female spouses.

In general, many participants did not feel that Air Force programs and policies adequately supported modern families with two working parents or female breadwinners, who may have a stay-at-home husband.[19] They expressed frustration that resources were largely designed to support a 1950s family model that included a stay-at-home wife and mother. While many noted that efforts were moving in the right direction, some still felt that there needed to be a paradigm shift to reflect the modern-day family and personal life situation.

Career Factors

Beyond family and personal life factors, we also asked female officers how elements of their Air Force career may influence their retention decisions. The career factors raised in our groups

---

[19] For a review of how the family structure has changed over the years, see Cohen (2015).

focused primarily on three areas: career path flexibility, ability to cross-train, and civilian opportunities. These are described in detail next.

Career Path Flexibility

More than half of the focus groups (52 percent) raised the inflexibility of career paths as a factor affecting whether female officers chose to remain in or leave the Air Force. Participants described the Air Force career pyramid as a rigid career path they must follow that allows for very little deviation and few alternatives. Female officers also perceived this strict career path to be somewhat incompatible with family and personal lives. In particular, balancing the demands of dual-military marriages and of children were viewed as difficult because of the rigidness of the Air Force career path. For example, one participant stated,

> I understand that there are certain things that leaders . . . need to learn to lead a larger organization, but the Air Force is rigid on what that looks like and doesn't entertain alternatives. So if your spouse has changed career paths, or you took the beta career, you know your opportunities for advancement are going to stop. So, do I waste my time doing this or do something else that gives me more opportunities for development? The Air Force is rigid with that kind of stuff and doesn't entertain alternatives. If they don't want me, fine, but don't get annoyed that women are not staying in—you can't have it both ways.

Similarly, another participated stated,

> In terms of joint spouses in your career field, the AF can do more to help. Some stress the pyramid and the pyramid doesn't fit everyone based on how it is configured. Maybe they need to have different pyramid types. They should have other options for those in the same career field.

Female officers expressed the desire for alternative career paths, such as part-time options that would involve such conditions as receiving less pay and serving additional years beyond 20 in order to receive retirement benefits. They felt that part-time options would allow female officers an option to remain in the Air Force with an improved work-life balance to support family needs. Additionally, participants mentioned that they would like to have more opportunities to take career-broadening assignments outside the career path pyramid, such as teaching at the U.S. Air Force Academy or a rotation with a civilian organization. For example, one participant commented,

> One of the things I've been thinking about that could be amazing, and this is just for the health care and not line side because that's totally different, but it would be amazing if we could use the VA and offer clinical rotation assignments at a federal type of facility as a health care worker. That can expand our experience and give us more assignment options that could potentially work better with personal work-life balance.

Many participants also stated that they would prefer to continue work in the technical aspects of their career fields without transitioning to the management roles and associated demands of senior leadership. For some female officers, this desire was related to not wanting to give up the technical work they enjoy, while for others it was connected to their perceptions of senior leadership having no work-life balance. For example, one participant stated,

> It would also be good to let people cap out at captain and just let people do their jobs at that level. Don't worry about making rank and leadership. Let them do a good job at that level. For pilots—if they told me I'm going to be a T6 instructor and work a 9–5 and stay a captain, I'd be like, sure, I'll definitely stay in! I'm going to work no matter what, even if I get out of the Air Force. The Air Force should acknowledge that they've invested in me and should keep me for that type of role, even if not for senior leadership.

A few participants suggested that a technical track be established to allow officers to specialize in their career fields without the pressures of senior leadership. For example, one participant commented,

> In the UK, there's a leadership track, or tactician, and stay and be really good at a job and make rank, more slowly, and you become a senior flyer, and we don't have that for any of our career fields in the Air Force.

A number of participants volunteered that an inflexible career path was the biggest factor influencing their decisions whether to stay in or leave the Air Force.

Ability to Cross-Train

Participants in 37 percent of focus groups raised female officers' inability to cross-train into other career fields (i.e., switch or change their career field) as a factor that influences retention decisions. Some participants described a desire to cross-train because they lack interest in their current career field. This was often a result of female officers having not received their preferred career field at commissioning and even after several years in the career field, remaining unhappy in the career field the Air Force had "chosen" for them. Other participants relayed experiences of not having received adequate information about what certain career fields entailed when having to provide precommissioning career field preferences. Once on the job and learning about the career field, some female officers found these careers did not match with their interests, personalities, or expectations.

Some female officers with joint spouses said they wanted to cross-train and join a career field more compatible with that of their spouses to improve colocation opportunities. Others noted additional personal reasons, such as wanting to cross-train into career fields that were less deployable or had a lower operational tempo so they could more easily have children or spend more time with their families. For example, one participant stated,

> Make it easier at the 10-, 11-year point—give the option to change career fields. . . . What we wanted at 18 or 20 years old is probably not what is appealing to us at 35 and if there are career fields that are more compatible with our lifestyle and not saying to become an F-16 pilot tomorrow . . . but something that is realistic—an acquisitions officer—and I could live in one of five places and I know I wouldn't deploy. But that's forbidden at this point—it's considered starting over. And if you're leading and you have skillset, forget it.

Female officers who had made attempts to cross-train noted that this was extremely difficult to do and that the Air Force does not provide information about how to pursue this. One participant stated,

> I've actually had people cross-train into my career field because they want to have kids. It's difficult for officers to cross-train. I can't get ahold of AFPC. . . . Me, as a personnelist, I'm not even getting information to tell people how to cross-train. I've heard things, but not sure what the regulations are. And how does that work with academy grads? There is so much unknown and no regulation on how to cross-train.

Some participants also described restrictions for cross-training when in career fields that are undermanned and unwilling to release officers to pursue opportunities in another career field. For example, one participant commented,

> I got into OSI [Office of Special Investigations] and right off the bat I figured I got in the wrong career field. I tried to cross-train but I was told no. I'm applying for others [career fields] but told no every time. I love the Air Force and want to be a part of it. I just don't like what I'm doing. People are stuck in career fields because the manning is so low.

A few focus group participants noted that they planned to separate specifically because they had not been allowed to cross-train into a new career field that was a better fit for their interests or lifestyle. Some female officers acknowledged that cross-training could affect their promotion potential and they would have to work their way up again, but still wanted to have that opportunity. One participant commented,

> Let people retrain. If you've been in for ten years, let them start at the bottom of the food chain again in a new career if they want to. Let them try. . . . Another friend I had, she was a pilot and her husband was a missileer. They can't be stationed together. She got out so she could live with her husband. The Air Force lost a great member because they wouldn't let her cross-train.

Civilian Opportunities

Some female officers believed the civilian workforce might provide more attractive opportunities than their Air Force careers. Participants in 43 percent of focus groups cited better civilian prospects as a factor in retention decisions, and this was across pay grade. Most comments about civilian opportunities noted higher civilian salaries as a reason for potentially leaving the Air Force, with these remarks centering on particular career fields (e.g., contracting, logistics, medical, pilots, legal) that participants believed were easily transferable to successful civilian careers.

Female officers also perceived some civilian jobs to be less stressful and require fewer hours in the office than Air Force careers. For example, one participant stated,

> I can make two times [as much] as a civilian doing the same thing with less stress. For any Fortune 500, they're making twice as much and they have a 9–5

27

job—and the grass is always greener, but I'm sure they don't get as many phone
calls in the middle of the night.

Beyond a potential 40-hour work week, participants perceived that some civilian jobs were likely to have more flexibility, including telework options and flexible hours, and would not require deployments. Some female officers mentioned that these aspects of civilian careers would help with family concerns and provide more time to spend with children.

A few participants also commented that, unlike Air Force career paths, civilian careers offered opportunities to continue in technical work rather than transitioning to a management track. This was attractive to some participants, who preferred the technical work of their career field and did not desire to promote into primarily management roles. For example, one participant stated,

So what I'm witnessing is females are leaving because they don't want to work
15-hour-a-day jobs. All the technical skills you'll get . . . stops at lower
levels. . . . After that, you're just a manager, if you stay it's because you love
management. . .

Work Environment Factors

We also asked female officers how their work environment might influence retention decisions. Key themes discussed in this area included the importance of leadership, female role models, mentoring, gender composition, sexual harassment and assault, and long work hours or shift work.

Leadership

We specifically asked participants how, if at all, leadership influences decisions regarding staying in or leaving the Air Force. Comments in this area particularly focused on the extent to which poor or "toxic" leadership can create a negative work environment and can reduce job satisfaction, motivation, and desire to stay in. For example, one participant described her thoughts as follows:

Really good leadership that's supportive. If you have good leadership, you're
more likely to stay in, and crappy leadership, more likely to get out. If it's a toxic
environment, that could be the tipping point.

Alternatively, other participants commented on their experiences of having a supportive leader and the positive impact it had on their experiences in the Air Force. In particular, for female officers who have children, having leaders who encouraged them to attend to various child care–related issues, including being supportive of things like needing to pump at work, helped them better balance their family and work demands. For example, one participant stated,

My commander, knowing [my spouse is also in the military] and I have all the
kids on my own, if I send him an email at 5 a.m., he tells me to go
home. . . . Your supervisor can really influence your situation and your decisions.

As noted earlier in this chapter, work-life balance is one of the key issues that participants raised as affecting their retention decisions. At the same time, having leaders who are not supportive or understanding of family needs helps contribute to a negative or toxic work environment. One participant commented,

> I have a friend and she had to pick up her kids and her female leader told her, "if the Air Force wanted you to have kids they would have issued them to you." That's not the type of statement anyone should have made. But it's maybe even worse because it was said by a female.

Finally, participants also noted the importance of commanders in influencing their career trajectories, including their officer performance reports and the assignments they receive. Participants commented that an unsupportive or bad leader can derail your career, influencing your decision to remain.

Female Role Models

Although we directly asked about the importance of leadership in general, 83 percent of focus groups also specifically raised the importance of having female role models in senior leadership positions, with many in male-dominated career fields commenting that they had never had a female commander. Furthermore, across groups, participants commented that they rarely see female leaders who are married with children. As a result, the perception is that it is not possible for women to both have a family and make senior leadership in the Air Force. For example, one participant stated,

> My O-6 is the first female I've seen at that level with a family. Most are divorced or single or don't have kids. It's sending a message. If you want to be Gen Grosso, what do you have to give up to get there? It's hard for us or me to say I can be in that position and still have a happy husband and a family when I don't see that reflected. I haven't seen a female group commander like me, I don't think, ever!

Several women did note that this was also a motivator to them to stay in the Air Force though, so that they could be that role model to other women. For example, one participant commented,

> I work at a place where there are pictures of historical commanders, and they all are generals. You see who has led command through time, and you look at it and there has never been a woman. So part of me not only wants to be a leader but to influence other women along the way.

Mentorship

Related to the importance of having role models, 56 percent of the focus groups raised the importance of mentorship and its influence on retention decisions. In particular, participants discussed the importance for career success of having a good mentor. However, many female officers commented that they did not have a mentor or know how to find a mentor. For example, one participant stated,

29

> I didn't do things right in the beginning, but having a mentor, I would have been a better officer early on if the Air Force had taken the time to mentor me.

One third of the groups also specifically discussed a desire to receive mentorship from successful females. In particular, they commented on wanting to have another female to talk with about how to best navigate an Air Force career along with having a family. Finding a female mentor was particularly difficult in certain career fields that were male dominated, however.

Gender Composition

We specifically asked participants about the influence of gender composition on work experiences and retention. For some participants, they were in career fields that tended to have more females, whereas other participants were in career fields that were male dominated (e.g., pilots, security forces, engineering). For those women in male-dominated career fields, they noted that they were used to being one of only a few women in their unit. Overall, participants had a mixed response regarding whether gender composition was important to them and influenced their retention decisions. For example, some participants commented that they liked being the only female. As one participant noted,

> It's not for everyone, but for me, I came into the military expecting to be the minority and work around mostly guys and be one of only 1 or 2 girls. Expectations may change based on career field, but it's not a retention consideration for me.

For others, though, the gender composition was an important influence on their experiences in the Air Force. For example, participants commented that, in male-dominated career fields in particular, they often faced sexism and the existence of an "old boy's network." This included feeling like they had to work harder to prove themselves and feeling like they were sometimes not treated equally because they were female. Participants brought up these issues in 94 percent of our focus groups. For example, one participant stated,

> As the only female in the squadron, you have to be tougher than the guys, and it sucks. And you pick up the pick axe and swing away and you cannot show weakness, especially as an officer.

Similarly, another participant commented,

> Maintenance is known as a man's career field, and a rough-and-tumble crowd. I was warned before commissioning that I would have a lot of hurdles being young and female. One captain told me I was pretty and wouldn't take me seriously. I had an old crusty chief say it was better before women were there.

Participants noted that these comments were not only from their peers, but they sometimes faced similar attitudes from leadership as well. For example, one participant stated,

> I was in a mentoring program, and a male lieutenant colonel sat with me and I was a first lieutenant. And, no kidding, that first meeting, he said don't let anyone lie to you, there is a glass ceiling for women and don't let anyone tell you otherwise. And, I'm not planning on changing that.

30

Female officers also described having to often walk a fine line in how they are perceived that male officers do not. If they are too nice or caring, they are not taken seriously, but if they are stern, they are considered a "bitch." Discussing this issue for women in the military, scholars have noted that women, particularly female leaders, are often seen as being less legitimate than men in military hierarchies. As a result, they often have to resort to using the power of their position to get people to do things, but this only further minimizes how others view their legitimacy as a leader (Lucas and Segal, 2012).

Finally, participants also commented that the gender composition was particularly important for having female officer role models and mentors along with a support network of friends. We discuss comments related to this issue in the previous section.

Sexual Harassment and Assault

Without our asking specifically about this issue, 37 percent of our focus groups raised sexual harassment and sexual assault as a critical concern. The majority of these comments focused on experiences of sexual harassment, particularly in male-dominated units and career fields. For example, one participant stated,

> When I've told people that I want to go to a fighter squadron, they say, "Oh, you need to grow a thicker skin because that sexual harassment stuff is all you're going to get, that attitude and that mentality." I don't want to do that because I get sick of being around that stuff all the time.

Some female officers also cited cases in which either they or individuals they knew had decided to leave specifically because of a sexual assault. Participants commented that female officers often do not want to report the incident, and instead decide to just separate. Participants also noted that these concerns were particularly heightened when deployed. For example, one participant noted, "I'm volunteering to deploy and my biggest fear is sexual assault."

Participants commented that they do see the Air Force taking steps to address the issues of sexual harassment and sexual assault. Some also noted having had a positive personal experience of leadership stepping in to stop an incident of sexual harassment. However, these issues persist in the Air Force and are particularly critical for women.

Long Work Hours and Shift Work

Participants in 85 percent of our focus groups also raised the issue of long hours or shift work playing a role in their retention decisions. Participants described often working 10- to 12-hour days and sometimes nights, which they felt often led to burnout. As was already discussed in a previous section, participants also described expectations of long hours and inflexible schedules negatively affecting their ability meet their family demands. For some, they noted this was the main reason they were going to get out. For example, one participant noted, "Work hours are so long and demanding. You see a lot of divorce. People don't see family, so for women who have a family, it's a challenge to balance." In addition, participants commented that the perception is that these hours only get longer and more demanding as rank increases. Therefore, for many, they were not sure that senior leadership was something they wanted to pursue. As one participant noted,

> As you go up, your hours are getting longer, so nothing is going to give. I would love to be a colonel one day, but that's working 20 hours a day, so no work-life balance.

Participants commented that these long hours were often the result of additional duties or undermanning in the unit. In addition, participants noted that expectations of what was required to keep progressing in one's career, such as obtaining an advanced degree, placed additional demands on their time.

For some career fields, such as missiles, shift-work schedules were also a challenging aspect of their job. Participants described needing to work 12-hour shifts, including night shifts, that were very difficult when they had children and particularly difficult if they were a single parent. For example, one participant stated, "As far as shift work, I've worked every holiday—not continuously, but I've missed every holiday and birthday at some point."

Broader Air Force and Military-Related Factors

The focus groups also discussed how several factors associated with the broader Air Force or general military structure influence retention decisions. In particular, we specifically asked focus group participants about how the number of deployments or PCS moves may influence retention decisions. However, in almost all focus groups, this issue was raised organically when asking about general factors related to retention decisions. In additional to deployments and PCS, participants also raised the importance of Air Force benefits and force reduction on retention decisions. We describe these in more detail next.

Benefits

When asked about factors that may influence retention of female officers, participants in 54 percent of our focus groups raised a number of Air Force benefits that they said are positive motivators for remaining in the service. Retirement benefits were the most frequently mentioned Air Force benefit related to retention. At the time of this study, active duty officers could receive a defined annuity benefit equal to 2.5 percent of their years in service multiplied by their retired pay base, but they had to serve in the military for at least 20 years. Participants commented that the promise of retirement benefits incentivizes many to remain in the Air Force for at least 20 years.

Potential changes to the retirement system, such as the blended retirement system outlined in FY 2016 NDAA (which would provide an option for service members to receive matching contributions to a Thrift Savings Plan and midcareer incentive pay, but reduce the amount of compensation for staying in for 20 years)[20] were met with mixed reactions. For example, one participant viewed potential changes with concern and stated,

> They are talking about changing the retirement system and 12 years and under, they are talking about changing it. I've already met my other goals, and staying in for 20 and give me stability, so if they change that—my incentive is gone. You're taking away what I signed up for 10 years ago!

Other participants considered having more options in a blended retirement system as a positive change. For example, one participant commented,

> Give more options for early retirement. . . . What about an option to get something at 15 years? Not full retirement, but something. I'd probably try to stay in til 15. Twenty is tough but 15 may be more realistic. Think about when you're going to get out at 20 years—you'll be 44 years old, and have to plan for a civilian career. . . . Is it going to be hard in your 40s to start at the bottom again? You could get out at an age where you are still young enough and need to work but you are much older than college grads. If I could get out at 15, I would definitely do that.

Female officers also emphasized the value of other Air Force benefits that encourage them to stay, including education (e.g., tuition assistance, GI Bill, Air University), health care (i.e., TRICARE), and housing (i.e., BAH and government housing options), among others.[21] One participant stated,

> Benefits. I know my salary wasn't as much as my civilian friends' salaries, but I got education benefits, a housing allowance, health care—that really weighed into my decision [to stay in the Air Force]. . . . If they took something away, whether that's salary, health care, housing, I would really have to consider [whether to stay in the Air Force].

While acknowledging that Air Force officers' salaries may be lower than their civilian counterparts, some participants noted that these types of benefits make up the difference in overall income. One participant stated,

> Retention is hard as well, because once the four years are up, they are swayed by higher-paying companies—student loans are expensive, and coming out of my degree I could've gotten a higher paying job, but I'll caveat that: The salary may be higher, but a lot of us in the military don't count the benefits we get, like our health care, a lot of the other nonmonetary value that we get from the military. So when you add all that up, we don't get that low of a salary compared to the civilian world, at least in engineering and computer science.

Female officers also mentioned the financial stability that comes with an Air Force salary and benefits, despite some career fields having opportunities for higher civilian salaries. A few

---

[20] For more details on changes resulting from the blended retirement system, which will go into effect January 1, 2018, see DoD (undated).

[21] For details on the various benefits provided to Air Force members, see Air Force Sergeants Association Division 4 (2017).

participants did note, however, that pay and housing allowances were sometimes inadequate in certain high-income locations, such as Washington, D.C., or Los Angeles. Participants raised very few comments related to bonus pay or similar incentives, and it is not clear whether these would have a significant impact on retention.

Overall, the variety of benefits that come with an Air Force career appeared to be the most positive motivator for staying in the Air Force past one's initial service commitment. This is also consistent with previous Air Force survey findings that show that for both males and females who intended to remain in the Air Force for at least 20 years, the top reasons for remaining in the Air Force were the retirement program, overall compensation and benefits package, and availability of medical care (AFPC, 2013; Olson, 2016).

PCS and Deployments

Prior research by the Military Leadership Diversity Commission (2011) found that female officers cited high frequency of deployments and a desire to settle in one location as key reasons for separating. Therefore, if not raised organically, which it almost always was, we asked participants specifically about how PCS and deployments might influence retention decisions. In nearly all of our focus groups, participants described PCS and deployments as key influencers on retention decisions. Participants described the impact of PCS and deployments primarily on two main areas: spouses and children.

Spousal issues related to PCS came up in 78 percent of the groups, and spousal issues with deployments came up in 81 percent of groups. As discussed in previous sections, participants had concerns about the negative effects on civilian spouse employment because of frequent PCS moves. For female officers with military spouses, their primary concern related to PCS was separation from their spouse when not colocated during the assignment process. Participants' concerns about deployments and spouses, detailed in earlier sections of this chapter, centered on issues related to civilian spouses having to serve as single parents during deployments and military couples' fear of being deployed on the same cycle and leaving children without either parent.

Child-related issues with PCS came up in 70 percent of the groups, and issues with deployments came up in 85 percent of groups. For example, participants mentioned concerns about children having to change schools regularly due to frequent PCS moves. For issues associated with deployments, participants noted that they felt guilt over separation from their children during deployments and missing important milestones in their children's lives.

To alleviate some of the problems associated with PCS moves, some participants suggested possible alternatives. These included options for a Permanent Change of Assignment at a base large enough to accommodate this, rather than a PCS. Participants generally thought less-frequent PCS moves would be beneficial for families.

In addition to the aforementioned problems and concerns that female officers raised related to PCS and deployment, some female officers in our groups noted positive aspects of PCS and deployments. Positive issues with PCS came up in 20 percent of the groups, and with deployment in 24 percent. These female officers noted that PCS moves provide opportunities to see new places and meet new people. Others felt that frequent moves resulted in their children becoming more resilient and having a greater cultural understanding. Some female officers without children noted, however, that their positive opinions of PCS and deployments could change after having children.

Force Reduction

A few participants, in 15 percent of focus groups, raised concerns about recent force reductions, where the Air Force cuts members to reduce manning levels. They noted that this affects decisions to stay in or leave the Air Force, saying that force reductions resulted in a loss of stability that they had expected their Air Force careers to provide. Some participants mentioned fears of not being able to remain in the Air Force for 20 years due to future shaping of the force, despite having goals to serve until retirement. Some female officers also noted that they felt that force reductions reflected a lack of commitment from the Air Force to its people, which diminished a feeling of commitment to the Air Force. For example, one participant stated,

> One of my strong considerations for getting out—stability and something to hold on to and they say the Air Force is your stability. But I'm on a RIF [reduction in force] board and there's no guarantee to stay until 20, so I might get out because the Air Force didn't provide the stability I needed.

Participants noted that force reductions can also result in undermanning issues, where there are fewer people to carry the workload. This "doing more with less" mentality came up frequently in these discussions, with female officers reporting the associated long hours that can negatively affect retention. One participant noted,

> After force reduction, the motto was "do more with less." And I went to greenbelt training and first thing they said, doing more with less doesn't work. It equals Band-Aid fixes and things start to crumble and the cracks get bigger and usually the women are the ones who give up.

Additionally, participants pointed out that undermanning issues associated with force reductions leave fewer people to share the deployment burden, potentially causing more-frequent deployments for individual officers.

Recently Established Air Force Programs/Policies

Focus group discussions also sought to gauge female officers' opinions about two recently established Air Force programs and policies: the updated maternity leave policy and the CIP.[22]

---

[22] It is important to note that these two changes to program and policy are not the only efforts the Air Force has instituted to help improve diversity among its ranks. Given time constraints when conducting the focus groups, it would not be possible to review all Air Force changes. Therefore, at the request of the study sponsors, these two efforts were selected as a specific focus because of their potential in helping address key retention factors for female officers.

Through this feedback, the research team aimed to assess whether this new policy and new program might have an effect on female officers' decisions about whether to stay in or leave the Air Force. The themes of this feedback are described here.

Updated Maternity Leave Policy

In early 2016, the Air Force extended maternity leave from six weeks of continuous, fully paid leave to 12, in compliance with new DoD-wide policy changes (Air Force, 2016).[23] Under the new Air Force policy, women can also defer fitness tests and deployments for one year after the birth of a child. Generally, participants' comments about this updated policy were positive. Female officers thought that the new policy is a step in the right direction to support women in the Air Force, and many felt that the previous leave of just six weeks was often not adequate. Participants mentioned that with the old policy, child care was sometimes difficult to arrange before the end of maternity leave and that a return to work at six weeks sometimes required babies to be sent to day care unvaccinated, which is often not permitted at child care facilities. Female officers also reported that the updated policy helps facilitate breastfeeding with less stress due to the longer leave, and accommodates difficult pregnancies or births, such as premature births or C-sections. For example, one participant stated,

> I think it [the updated maternity leave policy] was necessary—six weeks is not enough. I purposely stored extra leave so I didn't have to bring my unvaccinated child to day care. That helps our force and our family. I had a perfect textbook pregnancy and I think at six weeks when I needed to go back, I still wasn't ready—I needed eight weeks.

Female officers also discussed the deployment deferment as an improvement, decreasing early separation from children. Deferment of fitness tests was also seen as very positive, as some participants relayed incidents before this deferment policy in which they experienced injury from returning to physical training too soon after a difficult birth or C-section in order to pass fitness test requirements. Some noted that this deferment is not necessary for everyone, but it is good to have in place to protect those who do need it to prevent injuries.

While most female officers viewed the updated policy as an improvement, responses were mixed regarding whether this new policy might influence retention decisions. Some participants expressed concern over taking a longer maternity leave, how that would be perceived by leadership and peers, and whether a longer leave could negatively affect careers. For example, one participant stated,

> I was able to take advantage of it. My baby came just five days after they passed it, and I was able to take advantage of the full three months. It is situation- and person-dependent. I put pressure on myself to work from home or come back sooner to avoid the perception of a three-month vacation. Luckily the people I

---

[23] If medically necessary, a physician could also authorize extension of maternity leave beyond 12 weeks.

work with are more mature and understand how hard it is. It is important that leadership look out for the younger group to avoid that stigma.

Female officers also reported that leadership played a significant role in whether they were supportive of the extended leave policy and if female officers felt comfortable taking the full leave. One participant noted,

> I have a friend who has a baby who works in flight line–centric support operations. When she got pregnant, her leadership wanted to remove her from that position, so she had to fight very hard to stay in her position. It worked, but she struggled with choosing to take her 12 weeks of maternity leave because logistics is a fast moving field, and she knew that the guys would pass her if she stayed out that long.

Participants also mentioned concerns about how the extended maternity leave would affect Officer Performance Reports. This issue was of particular concern for career fields that are statistics-driven, such as Judge Advocate General, or for pilots who will lose additional flying time. Female officers in these career fields noted they may be less likely to take the full maternity leave because of the fear of negative career effects. A few participants commented that while they generally viewed the updated leave policy as positive, they had concerns about resentment from male peers related to the stigma of a "baby vacation" and having to cover the workload or deployment for female officers resulting from this updated policy.

In addition to this change in maternity leave policy, some female officers raised the issue of extending paternity leave. Not only could this serve to assist mothers with caring for newborns, but some felt that this could also somewhat reduce the stigma associated with female officers taking maternity leave because both parents would have updated leave policies and be sharing more of the child care duties. Additionally, participants noted that extended adoption leave would be beneficial to female officers.

Career Intermission Program

The CIP allows a service member to take a onetime transition from active duty service to the Individual Ready Reserve with partial pay, for up to three years, before returning to active duty to meet personal or professional needs outside of the service. Once they rejoin active duty, service members are then required to serve two months of active duty service for every month of CIP participation (Pub. L. 110-417; Pub. L. 113-291). The program requires applicants to apply and be approved for participation.

When we asked focus group participants about the CIP, understanding and awareness of the program itself varied. Some female officers were aware of the program but were not clear on its details. Other participants, more often those who were more junior officers, had never heard of the CIP at all. Overall, many participants felt as though the program is not well advertised across the Air Force, and that it is very difficult to get selected for the CIP due to the small number of opportunities. The CIP was originally a pilot program with limited slots. The FY 2016 NDAA lifted the pilot status of the program, however, opening the number of service members who can participate.

Once CIP was described to focus group members who were not aware of the program, most felt that they were glad CIP exists and thought that it could be beneficial. For example, having access to CIP in the case of an extended family emergency, such as needing to care for an immediate family member with a terminal illness, could help female officers. Some participants also noted that if used for civilian employment or education, the CIP could give officers new perspectives to bring back to the Air Force.

Despite these potential benefits, most focus group participants believed it would have little bearing on retention and were skeptical that it would not have negative career effects. Some female officers believed that participation in CIP could be viewed differently by leadership and peers depending on how CIP participants used their time away from the Air Force. Many female officers felt that if CIP participants used the time to further their education or for some other type of career development, they could be viewed as an asset when returning to active duty. Alternatively, if they used CIP to spend time with family or have children, this may be viewed negatively and affect their careers in a negative way. For example, one participant stated,

> Men are going to have to be the ones to [participate in the CIP] first. As soon as women do that to leave and have kids, people will think this is a women's program so they can have kids. Not for a mission or religious trip or going back to school, something like that, but if it starts out as women taking it—it'll be a women's program and male counterparts and leaders will see it as a derogatory negative thing and that you left and played mom for three years.

Focus group participants also perceived that officers who intended to use CIP for education or career development would be selected for the program over officers who want to use CIP to be home with their children.

Additionally, female officers had concerns about being able to remain competitive in their Air Force careers after significant time off. Some participants mentioned potential problems with staying up to date with technology advances while away from the job or losing technical skills. For example, pilots generally did not view the CIP as a feasible option because of the impacts of being out of the aircraft for an extended period of time. One participant stated,

> [The CIP] seems like a trap . . . If I stay in, I'm going to board this summer. I wouldn't be working and I'd come back at the wrong time and wouldn't be competitive at boards if I did that program. For pilots, for flyers, you will lose all your currencies.

Female officers also found the CIP's double-time service commitment to be a disincentive to participation. Some mentioned fears of not wanting to return to the Air Force after experiencing civilian life, although many noted that an equal time commitment for time away from the Air Force rather than a double time commitment would make the program more attractive.

Summary

Focus groups with female officers about factors they consider when deciding whether to remain in or separate from the Air Force centered on four key areas: (1) family and personal matters, (2) career, (3) work environment, and (4) broader Air Force and military-related issues. For family and personal factors, themes focused primarily on children, pregnancy, breastfeeding, spouses, and dating. Career-related factors included issues concerning career path flexibility, the ability to cross-train, and opportunities in the civilian sector. Focus group participants also discussed retention factors related to their work environment, including leadership, female role models, mentoring, gender composition of units, sexual harassment and assault, and long work hours or shift work. Finally, participants also discussed factors related to aspects of the broader Air Force or military structure, including benefits, PCS and deployments, and recent force reductions. Female officers also provided feedback on two recently established Air Force policies and programs: the updated maternity leave policy and the CIP.

4. Conclusion and Recommendations

Our focus groups with female Air Force officers identified factors in four main areas that are important considerations when deciding to remain in or separate from the Air Force. All focus groups discussed family or personal factors as critical to their decisions, including the importance of children, spouses, dating, pregnancy, breastfeeding, and other issues related to officers' personal lives. The importance of these family-related factors is consistent with the findings from recent Air Force retention surveys, which also found that maintaining work-life balance and meeting family commitments were top influencers for leaving or intending to leave. For female officers, compatibility with a spouse's career or job and joint-spouse considerations were also top influencers from the survey findings (AFPC, 2013; Olson, 2016).

In addition to family-related factors, female officers in our focus groups identified career-related factors that influenced their decisions, including perceived career path inflexibility, a lack of ability to cross-train into another career field, and the appeal of better civilian opportunities. Female officers also discussed the importance of the overall work environment. This included the impact of leadership on the organizational climate and the ability to have work-life balance, the availability of female role models and mentors, experiences of sexism and sexual harassment, incidents or fears of sexual assault, and long work hours.

There were also broader factors related to having an Air Force or military career that were important, such as the impact of frequent PCS and deployments on family. Military benefits, such as health care, education, and retirement pension, were identified as the most positive motivator to retention, which aligns with findings from recent Air Force surveys.

It is important to note that, in many cases, these factors were interrelated in that certain characteristics of the Air Force career or work environment were undesirable themselves, but also then affected family issues. For example, frequent PCS moves affected issues related to spouse separation and children. The rigidness of the career pyramid affected career broadening interests, as did an ability to adequately address family needs while still climbing the ladder to senior leadership. In other words, many decisions to separate from the Air Force for female officers seemed to depend on the ability of the Air Force to support career progression and having a family or personal life at the same time.

Recommendations

Here, we provide recommendations focused on addressing the key factors raised in the focus groups that were important considerations for female officer retention decisions. These recommendations are based on potential policy or program changes identified by the research team that may be able to help address the various retention factors raised in our focus groups.

They also reflect recommendations for improvements raised by focus group participants themselves. It is important to note, however, that we do not provide separate recommendations for every factor mentioned within the groups; instead, we focus on recommendations designed to address the most-prominent themes or that may have broad effects across several key retention factors. For example, increased career flexibility was identified as important not just for career satisfaction but also for meeting family needs.

Table 4.1 provides an overview of these proposed initiatives and how they map onto the retention factors identified from our focus groups in the previous chapter. In general, these initiatives fall into three broad categories of action: (1) dissemination of additional information or education, (2) enhancements to existing programs or policies, and (3) broader structural changes to the personnel system.

Table 4.1. Initiatives for Addressing Barriers to Female Officer Retention

Focus Area	Initiatives
Family/Personal Factors	
Children	• Expand subsidized child care options and available CDC hours* • Increased paternity and adoption leave*
Breastfeeding support	• Ensure women are provided a designated nursing facility or private room for pumping*
Civilian spouse support	• Ensure spouse support programs and initiatives are inclusive of male spouses
Military spouse support	• Consider a couple's parental status and needs in deployment policy • Identify an interservice liaison to coordinate cross-service spouse assignments
Career-Related Factors	
Career field knowledge	• Provide tools for educating precommissioning officers on career field options, including differences in locations, deployments, spouse compatibility, etc.
Cross-training	• Provide a structure and related policy for allowing more cross-training opportunities
Career flexibility	• Offer a separate technical career track • Expand and raise awareness of the CIP* • Provide flexibility for transferring into and back from the Air Force Reserve
Work Environment Factors	
Leadership and family	• Provide education for leaders on creating positive work-life balance
Leadership and sexual harassment/assault	• Provide education for leaders on prevention of a sexist work environment
Role modeling and mentoring	• Provide opportunities for women-focused panels/forums
Broader AF/Military Factors	
PCS/assignment process	• Explore options for reducing the frequency of PCS* • Explore a more decentralized assignment process to allow officers more autonomy in assignments

* An initiative mentioned in proposed DoD changes from Defense Secretary Ashton Carter for developing the Force of the Future (DoD, 2015b; DoD, 2016a; DoD, 2016b).

In several cases, the initiatives we identified are also consistent with already proposed changes for DoD presented by former Defense Secretary Ashton Carter as part of his Force of the Future initiative (noted in Table 4.1). Specifically, in 2015, Carter assumed office and announced his intent to pursue reforms to personnel systems and talent management across DoD (DoD, 2015a). The specific changes proposed through the Force of the Future initiative were publicized in three tranches. The first tranche was announced in November 2015 and included an initiative to increase the size of the CIP. As described in Chapter 3, this program began as a pilot program to be implemented across the services in 2009, and it allows service members to take a sabbatical from service for up to three years as part of the Individual Ready Reserve. Under the Force of the Future initiative, the program's pilot status was eliminated, and the program was expanded to increase utilization and duration. The second tranche, announced in January 2016, included multiple changes to address the needs of military families (DoD, 2016a). This tranche also included the establishment of a 12-week paid maternity leave standard for all active duty service members and certain Reserve component members, doubling the maternity leave that had been allowed by the Air Force. We already assessed reactions to this change in maternity leave policy as part of our study. The third tranche, announced in June 2016, included multiple proposed changes that would require legislation before implementation (DoD, 2016b).

In the sections to follow, we discuss each of the proposed initiatives outlined in Table 4.1 in more detail.

Family/Personal Focused Initiatives

The first two initiatives in Table 4.1 address focus group participants' concerns related to meeting children's needs. In particular, the first initiative focuses on expanding subsidized child care options and available CDC hours to address concerns regarding accessible and high-quality child care. Additional child care options that the Air Force can explore could include expanding the Family Child Care program, which offers in-home child care and was mentioned in our focus groups as a beneficial program. The second initiative related to children focuses on increased paternity and adoption leave. This was raised by some focus group participants when discussing the expansion of maternity leave to help meet family needs and to help dispel the female stigma associated with maternity leave. Variations of these initiatives were already proposed as part of the Force of the Future actions.[24] Additional initiatives to help meet children's needs are also

---

[24] Force of the Future actions included the following:

- extension of CDC hours to a 14-hour minimum. These 14 hours must overlap with the normal working shifts of service members by at least two hours. Further, children may receive up to 12 hours of subsidized care each day. Explore additional child care options to improve access and usability.
- request for congressional action to expand paternity leave from the standard of ten days to a new standard of 14 days and expand adoption leave for one service member to three weeks, and for dual military couples to also provide two weeks of adoption leave for the second service member.

included as part of other initiatives described later addressing career flexibility and work-family balance.

Focus group participants also raised concerns related to breastfeeding and being able to have a private space to pump once back at work. This initiative has also been addressed as part of the Force of the Future actions, with a focus on establishing standards for modifying or installing mother's rooms at each military installation. This includes installation or modification of mothers' rooms at all facilities at which more than 50 women are regularly assigned. Current Air Force policy also requires that women have a private space in which to pump (AFI 44-102). However, based on our focus group findings in which participants described difficulties in being provided accommodations for pumping, we would recommend that commanders be educated about the importance of following current policy and ensuring that women are provided a private space for pumping at smaller facilities that may not have a designated mother's room (e.g., private office).

Finally, nearly all groups discussed the impact that spouses can have on retention. For those female officers with civilian spouses, their partners often have difficulty transferring jobs or finding new employment with each PCS-related move. This is often made more challenging when Air Force spouse programs are not perceived as supportive or inclusive of male spouses, including during deployments. To help address some of these issues, we recommend that the Air Force review the effectiveness of currently utilized job placement programs and ensure that spouses are aware of and connected to these existing resources and programs. In addition, the Air Force should ensure that spouse support programs under their purview are designed to be inclusive of male spouses as well as females (e.g., include more male-oriented activities or designate a nontraditional spouse as Key Spouse).

For military spouses, the biggest issue raised was the potential for long periods of separation because of deployments or incompatible assignments. These dual-military spouse issues are particularly important for female officers, given that 34 percent of married female officers are married to an active duty Air Force spouse, and 3 percent are married to an active duty spouse in another service. By comparison, only 6 percent of married male officers are married to an active duty Air Force spouse, and fewer than 1 percent are married to an active duty member in another service.[25] It was beyond the scope of this study to examine the functioning and effectiveness of the Air Force's current joint-spouse program, including statistics on the number of dual-service couples who are actually separated through deployments or assignments and how often. However, the importance of this issue across our focus groups suggests that the Air Force may want to re-examine its current joint-spouse program and look for ways to improve the ability to keep Air Force families together. We note that since completion of this study, the Air Force has already taken some steps in this direction. In September 2016, as part of their new set of diversity and inclusion initiatives, they are requiring that the commander of AFPC sign off on

---

[25] Air Force personnel data for August 2016 provided to RAND by the Air Force Personnel Center.

any assignments that result in involuntary separation of dual-military families (Secretary of the U.S. Air Force, 2016).

In terms of additional specific initiatives to pursue, separation for dual-military couples can be particularly challenging when children are involved and both spouses are sent to deploy at the same time. In contrast, some dual-military couples who do not have children report actually wanting to deploy at the same time. Although there is an attempt to consider parental status and needs informally along with the needs of the Air Force when determining deployment schedules for dual-military couples, incorporating this consideration into policy could provide further benefit. Additionally, policy already exists to try to colocate joint spouses when possible. However, this process can be particularly difficult for cross-service spouses. Therefore, exploring additional mechanisms for further facilitating this process, such as liaison duties focused on coordinating cross-service assignments, could help improve some of the separation issues. Such liaison duties could even be incorporated into existing roles, but providing further structure and policy for such activities would better establish this coordination.

Career-Focused Initiatives

In terms of addressing barriers related to the Air Force career, the first initiative presented in Table 4.1 is focused on providing additional education for precommissioning officers on career field options. Although not the only factor considered in assignments, individual preferences are an important element in determining which Air Force specialties incoming officers are assigned. Therefore, limited or inaccurate information regarding different career fields may bias preferences. Importantly, career field choices have an effect not only on future job interest but also on compatibility with spouses (i.e., one career field may have limited assignment opportunities at locations where a spouse's career field has many, leading to frequent separation) and on children, all of which are important retention factors. A key strategy for addressing these issues early on is to ensure that cadets are educated regarding their different career field options, including differences in potential assignment locations, spouse career compatibility, operations tempo, and other career field demands. This could be done through additions to current career field material that is provided as a resource or through the creation of new tools (e.g., an interactive app) that could help guide cadets toward career fields that best align with their interests and life goals.

In addition to providing additional resources to help female officers make informed initial career field choices, the ability to cross-train or "recore" later in one's career into another career field was also raised in our focus groups as a way to help address both a lack of interest in one's career field and perceived incompatibility with family needs (e.g., incompatibility with a spouse's career or the care of a young child). Currently, cross-training or recoring already takes place for some career fields (e.g., Nuclear and Missile Operations) and in certain individual circumstances. However, cross-training is not a common practice across all career fields and is subject to broader Air Force considerations, including career field manning and the ability for the

Air Force to realize its return on training investment. Therefore, providing such opportunities may not be realistic in all career fields or for all officers. However, the Air Force could benefit from exploring ways to provide additional cross-flow or recoring opportunities where appropriate and developing a structured process and related policy for authorizing such changes. This should also include providing information to officers on the existence of any such opportunities and how to apply or navigate the process of cross-training. As noted in our focus group findings, many of our participants commented that there is a general lack of information on opportunities to cross-train or how one would apply to cross-train.

Another key theme that emerged in our focus groups was frustration with what was perceived as a rigid career pyramid that was often incompatible with family and personal interests. For example, some participants noted a desire to continue doing the technical work of their Air Force specialty instead of an interest in taking on a more managerial role. Others were not interested in passing through the various requirements for making senior leadership ranks, particularly due to perceptions of incompatibility between the time requirements of being a senior leader and having a family or the resulting continual separation from their family, but did express a continued desire to serve their country and remain in the Air Force. One option to address these concerns would be to explore the possibility of creating a more technical track that would be separate from the traditional leadership career track. This would require a dramatic change in many aspects of the current personnel management systems for officers, so there would be many considerations the Air Force would need to explore prior to implementation. However, the addition of such a track would provide more career flexibility for Air Force officers and may help address some of the issues related to meeting family needs and personal interests raised in our groups.

Related to career flexibility, the CIP was a specific program raised with focus group participants because of its goal to provide Airmen with an opportunity to take a break from active duty service. Findings from our focus groups showed that many female officers were not aware of or did not fully understand the CIP, however. Once they learned about it, they felt it had the potential to be beneficial, but were also wary of potential negative effects on their careers. Therefore, raising awareness of CIP and participant outcomes will be important to the effectiveness of the program. A permanent and expanded CIP that has a greater number of slots open for participation will also be beneficial to some female officers in providing an avenue for addressing personal or family needs for a brief period of time. This expansion of the CIP and elimination of it as a pilot program was one of the actions outlined in the Force of the Future initiative, and its pilot status was lifted as part of the FY 2016 NDAA, increasing the number of service members who can participate.[26]

Consistent with the CIP, participants raised a desire to have the option of taking a break from active duty so they could pursue other career interests, such as getting an advanced degree or

---

[26] Congressional authority for career intermission pilot programs (CIP) was only extended through calendar year 2019 under the fiscal year 2015 National Defense Authorization Act (Pub. L. 113-291, 2014).

meeting family needs. However, many participants also noted that they did not want to completely divorce themselves from their current work because of concerns that they would lose critical skills or not keep up with technological advances if they fully stepped out of the Air Force for even a short period of time. One option to address this concern and still allow officers greater flexibility in their career paths would be the development of a program similar to CIP that would allow officers to transfer into the Reserve Component for a limited number of years and then transfer back to active duty. This aligns with the idea of developing a true "continuum of service" for Air Force members. As with the CIP, the Air Force would need to consider how best to transfer officers back to active duty from the Reserves to ensure that their career progression would not be negatively affected. Decisions would also have to be made regarding how many individuals could be involved in such a program and how it would affect future promotions and manning in both the active duty and Reserve side. Therefore, this type of program would need careful consideration before implementation to ensure that there were not significant unintended consequences.

Work Environment Factors

The first two initiatives aimed at addressing factors related to the broader work environment focus on educating leaders about their role in creating a positive work-life balance and organizational climate free of sexism. Our focus groups identified the importance of leadership on their career experiences, particularly the ability to address family needs that are often more likely to fall on women. Participants stressed that leaders should recognize that the hours they stay in the office will influence the hours their staff work and that providing schedule flexibility (e.g., allowing telework or making sure officers can pick up a sick child) is important for quality of life and for helping officers better balance family and work demands. Similarly, many officers reported still experiencing an "old boy's network" and sexist remarks. Leaders must consider the extent to which their actions and the actions of others under their command may contribute to those experiences, and they must ensure that it is addressed. Thus, as a tangible action to work toward this goal, we recommend education for leaders on how to improve these aspects of the work environment they oversee. We acknowledge that education and training alone is not always sufficient to change leadership behavior, however. A larger culture shift from the top down would be needed to significantly and comprehensively change leader behavior in this area.

A final potential initiative for improving the work environment for female officers is focused on trying to provide more opportunities for women-focused panels or forums. Participants in our focus groups noted that they rarely see women in senior leader positions, particularly women who are married and have children. Therefore, many assume that being a senior Air Force leader and having a family are not compatible. In addition, finding other women to talk with who could provide mentorship on how to balance work and family was difficult. Participants mentioned Air Force–sponsored conferences and forums that were focused on discussing female issues and bringing women together that they found particularly helpful. Providing more of these

46

opportunities across a larger number of bases could help continue to connect female officers to one another. Such efforts may be particularly important for women in male-dominated career fields.

Broader AF/Military Factors

The final set of initiatives in Table 4.1 is focused on addressing female officers' concerns about the impact of frequent PCS on children, spouses, and personal lives. First, although it would require congressional approval, exploring options for allowing officers to delay a move for family reasons would provide some degree of flexibility related to the impact of PCS. This type of initiative was also one of the actions recently proposed as part of the Force of the Future efforts.[27]

The second initiative we propose involves exploring the utilization of a more decentralized assignment process or avenues for allowing officers to have more influence over their assignments. Airmen Development Plans are already used as a tool for officers to communicate their individual preferences (AFI 36-2640). However, participants noted that they often have little insight into what assignments are available in the first place and do not know what they should specify in their development plan. Providing officers more insight into available assignments and an ability to note those preferences directly or even apply to a range of assignments that work best for them could provide officers a greater sense of control over their careers and ability to balance competing personal needs (e.g., colocation with a joint spouse, stability for children, career-broadening opportunities). It is important to note that this type of initiative would require significant changes in how officers are managed today and would need considerable thought before implementation—changes in the assignment system would have far-reaching impacts on other aspects of officer career management.

Implementation Framework

The initiatives presented in Table 4.1 vary in their difficulty to implement and in their potential to affect female officer retention in the Air Force. Therefore, to aid the Air Force in thinking about the best way to move forward with any of these proposed initiatives, we provide a framework in Figure 4.1 to help identify which initiatives the Air Force may want to prioritize and which initiatives may need further study prior to implementation. The figure categorizes each proposed initiative based on its difficulty to implement and potential for impact on female officer retention in the Air Force. We define implementation difficulty based on the relative complexity of implementation (e.g., potential for unintended consequences due to required changes in other personnel management systems or policies). It is likely that initiatives that are

---

[27] The specific Force of the Future recommendation is as follows: Amendment to Title 10 authorities so service members could be allowed to remain at a station of choice for family reasons. Service members may postpone a PCS to address family needs in exchange for an additional active duty service obligation.

more complex to implement will also require more time to do so effectively. We base potential for impact on the number of retention factors an initiative may be able to address or the prominence of the retention factor among our focus groups.

Those initiatives falling in the lower right quadrant, which are easier to implement and have higher potential for impact, could be considered *quick wins*. Those initiatives falling in the upper right quadrant, which are more difficult to implement because of required structural and policy changes but still have higher potential for impact, are most likely to create *enduring systematic change*. Finally, we consider those initiatives falling in the lower left quadrant, which are easier to implement but likely to have lower impact, to be *contributors to incremental change*. Relative to other initiatives, these contributors to incremental change are not as complex to implement but also are not likely to have a sizable impact in and of themselves on female officer retention because of their focus on a single or narrower issue. However, they can still play a role in improving the overall Air Force environment and support for female officers.

Figure 4.1. Implementation Framework

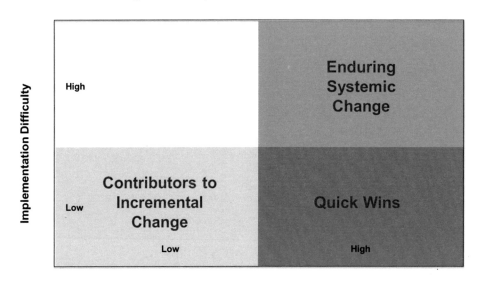

Potential for Impact

We discuss our assessment of which initiatives fall into each quadrant in the following sections. To gauge the validity of our initiatives and their placement in this framework, the research team also consulted with four senior RAND researchers possessing a rich expertise in Air Force personnel processes and systems. The researchers were presented with our proposed initiatives and their placement in the framework. We then held discussions by phone or in person to review the initiatives, their feasibility, and their placement within the framework. We incorporated comments from these experts into our final recommendations.

Quick Wins

There are three initiatives we would consider potential *quick wins:*

- Expand subsidized child care options and available CDC hours.
- Provide tools for educating precommissioning officers on career field options, including differences in locations, deployments, spouse compatibility, etc.
- Provide a structure and related policy for allowing more cross-training opportunities.

Based on our focus group findings, we believe these initiatives have the potential for higher impact on female officer retention and are less difficult to implement relative to other proposed initiatives (i.e., less complex with no significant potential for unintended consequences). In particular, extension of CDC hours and expansion of child care options were raised across our focus groups and could have a significant impact on the ability of officers to better balance the demands of an Air Force career and family needs. Providing increased education on career field options and providing greater structure, policy, and information for cross-flow opportunities can help address several of the different career- and family-related factors raised in our groups with no need for some of the more complex structural changes required by other initiatives.

Enduring Systemic Change

There are five initiatives that we would describe as contributing to *enduring systemic change:*

- Expand and raise awareness of the CIP.
- Explore options for reducing the frequency of PCS.
- Explore a more decentralized assignment process to allow officers more autonomy in assignments.
- Offer a separate technical career track.
- Provide flexibility for transferring into and back from the Reserve Component.

These initiatives are much more complex to implement because they require both policy and structural changes to the broader Air Force personnel system that would have consequences for various aspects of the officer personnel management system. Therefore, these initiatives would need to be examined more fully before implementation (e.g., modeling, pilot programs) to ensure that there would not be significant unintended consequences and that they would actually achieve the goal of helping address some of the barriers identified in our focus groups. Many of these changes would also require congressional action. However, we believe that these initiatives also have higher potential for affecting female officer retention because they would help address multiple retention factors raised in our focus groups by allowing greater career flexibility to meet both personal and family needs.

Contributors to Incremental Change

Finally, there are eight initiatives we think are *contributors to incremental change:*

- Ensure women are provided a designated nursing facility or private room for pumping.
- Increase paternity and adoption leave.
- Provide education for leaders on creating positive work-life balance.
- Provide education for leaders on prevention of a sexist work environment.
- Ensure spouse support programs and initiatives are inclusive of male spouses.
- Consider a joint couple's parental status and needs in deployment policy.
- Identify an interservice liaison to coordinate cross-service spouse assignments.
- Provide opportunities for women-focused panels/forums.

These initiatives are not difficult to implement but are not likely in and of themselves to have as sizable an impact on female officer retention as other proposed initiatives because they tend to focus on a single issue or concern raised in our groups. However, they can still play a role in improving the overall Air Force environment and support for female officers.

Although we include education for leaders on creating positive work-life balance and preventing a sexist work environment as contributors to incremental change, we want to acknowledge the significant importance of good leadership on the well-being of those under their command. Arguably, having consistent, supportive leaders focused on meeting the needs of their people and ensuring a positive command climate could be considered to have a much stronger potential effect on female officer retention. As noted, we recommend education for leaders as a tangible action to work toward this goal, but we recognize that education and training are not always sufficient to change leadership behavior. A larger culture shift from the top down would be needed to significantly and comprehensively change leader behavior in this area. If fully implemented, this could then contribute to enduring systemic change.

Further Evaluation of Proposed Initiatives

It is important to note that the findings in this study are suggestive. They are limited in that they rely on information generated through group discussions. Therefore, the true degree to which these proposed initiatives would impact female officer retention is still unknown. Additionally, many of the proposed initiatives are likely to also benefit male officers. However, it was beyond the scope of this study to conduct focus groups with male officers, so we do not know the extent to which this might be the case. Furthermore, it was beyond the scope of this study to analyze the changes necessary for each of the proposed initiatives, especially those that would require more complex structural and policy changes. Particularly for those initiatives that could be costly and difficult to implement, the Air Force could benefit from first trying to empirically determine which of the proposed initiatives are likely to have the most impact. For some initiatives, this could be done through implementation of a pilot program that could be evaluated for effectiveness. Other potential methods include a choice experiment, where respondents receive a survey and are presented with a series of retention decisions that have varying circumstances attached to them. By asking the respondents what they would do in the hypothetical scenarios, such a survey could get closer to measuring the effect that circumstances have on retention (though its validity would depend on self-reported preferences, rather than actual decisions). At a minimum, those initiatives that are high on implementation difficulty would need to be more fully examined prior to implementation because of their potential to also have unintended consequences (e.g., modeling of the impact of changes on relevant aspects of the officer personnel management system).

Summary

We were able to identify a few *quick win* initiatives that we believe have higher potential for impact and lower implementation difficulty. The initiatives likely to have the most effect on retention, however, would require significant structural and policy changes. These initiatives would need to be more fully examined prior to implementation because of their potential to have unintended consequences on other aspects of the current officer personnel management system. We also identified a set of initiatives that focus on addressing more-specific issues raised in our focus groups that, although not likely to significantly improve retention on their own, can contribute to improving the overall Air Force environment and support for female officers. In addition to the proposed initiatives in this chapter, it is also important to note that military benefits (e.g., health care, education, retirement pension) were identified as one of the key positive motivators for staying in the Air Force. Therefore, changes to these benefits should be made with caution, including changes to BAH, which was called out specifically in our focus groups. Finally, many of the proposed initiatives described in this chapter are also likely to benefit retention for male officers, who face some of the same challenges (although perhaps to a different degree). Thus, these initiatives may help address any unnecessary barriers for retaining talent across the Air Force, but particularly for women.

As the Air Force moves forward with making changes to improve retention of the force, and of female officers in particular, monitoring the effects of these changes will be important. This can be done through current Air Force retention surveys or follow-up focus groups or feedback panels. This will help ensure that any new initiatives are having their desired effect and help highlight continuing or new areas that may need to be addressed.

Appendix A. Previous Research on Barriers to Female Officer Retention

Our research team began this study with the understanding that women are underrepresented among the Air Force's senior leadership compared with their representation within the lower ranks. A large contributor to this underrepresentation is that women tend to leave the active duty Air Force at higher rates than men. As we identified the different factors that influence female officers to remain in or separate from the active duty Air Force—family and personal issues, career, work environment, and broader Air Force and military issues—we did so with the tacit awareness that current retention challenges for women have historical underpinnings that date back decades.

To provide some context, women have served in the U.S. military since the Revolutionary War, albeit in an informal fashion (see Sandhoff, Segal, and Segal, 2010). With the formation of the Army and Navy Nurse Corps in World War I, official roles for women were finally created. Women then served in all specialties starting in World War II, save direct combat. The Women's Armed Services Integration Act of 1948 "legalized a continued presence of women in the armed forces, but excluded them from combat missions on aircraft and naval vessels and placed a 2 percent cap on the overall representation of women in the military. In 1967, this ceiling was removed, but women remained less than 2 per cent of the force" (Sandhoff, Segal, and Segal, 2010, p. 124). The transition to an all-volunteer force in 1973 then began to increase the presence of women in the military further (Sandhoff, Segal, and Segal, 2010).

One well-known model for explaining the degree and nature of women's participation in the military focuses on the role of military, social, and cultural variables (Segal, 1995). Specifically, the model posits that less-secure societies with shortages of qualified men may elect to increase women's military roles during times of national emergency. Segal (1995) cites the examples of Germany and the United Kingdom in World War II, with the former conscripting women into what were nominally labeled "civilian jobs" and the latter conscripting women into both military and civilian service. Additionally, Segal notes that much has changed in the United States since the transition to an all-volunteer force in 1973, such as "a mushrooming of attention to women's current and past military contributions." Yet, she states that the military is the most prototypically masculine of all social institutions. Therefore, "for women to participate, either the military has to be perceived (by policymakers and the populace) as transformed to make it more compatible with how women are (or are perceived to be) or women have to be perceived as changing in ways that make them seemingly suited to the military" (p. 758). Recent research by Iskra and colleagues (2002) added a fourth dimension to the model that focuses on politics, with the idea that female participation in the military also depends on such factors as the "political ideology of those in power, and subsequent public policies regarding minorities and women"

(Iskra et al., 2002, p. 790). Thus, as female participation in the military has increased, trying to gain a better understanding of the experiences of women in the military and the effect of different military policies and practices on these experiences has received considerable attention across the decades.

According to DoD 2015 statistics, women composed 15.5 percent of total DoD active duty members (15.1 percent of enlisted members and 17 percent of officers). In the Air Force, specifically, women composed 18.8 percent of enlisted members and 20.3 percent of officers (DoD, 2015a). When looking at female Air Force officers, who are the topic of this study, Air Force Personnel data from August 2016 show that female officers make up 21.1 percent of officers in pay grades O-1 through O-5, but only 13.9 percent of officers at the O-6 level, and only 7.5 percent of officers at Brigadier General (O-7) or higher. In terms of marriage status, 58 percent of female Air Force officers are married, 33 percent are single, and 8 percent are divorced. For married female officers, 34 percent are married to another active duty Air Force member, and 3 percent are married to an active duty member in another service; for married male officers, only 6 percent are married to another active duty Air Force member, and fewer than 1 percent are married to an active duty member in another service.[28]

To provide additional context for our study of female Air Force officer retention, in the following sections of this appendix, we highlight previous research that has tried to gain a better understanding of gender differences in military retention and the different variables that may help explain why female retention tends to lag behind that of men. We also highlight relevant research on gender differences and retention in the civilian sector. It is important to note that this review is not intended as a comprehensive review of all retention literature; rather, it is intended to provide highlights of prior research particularly relevant to this study.

Prior Research on Gender Differences in Military Officer Retention

Given that the Air Force's interest is to maximize the return on its training investment, premature personnel separation represents a significant resource drain to be minimized. In terms of gender diversity, it also represents a barrier to increasing female representation in Air Force senior leaders. The definition of premature separation can vary, however. In broad terms, it can be categorized as individuals separating *before* the expiration of their service commitment or contract, or as individuals separating *after* the expiration of their service commitment, at which point they have no obligation to continue serving but the Air Force would likely prefer that they do.

Officers incur an Active Duty Service Commitment (ADSC) upon commission, selection for specialized training, PCS, or a number of other reasons that require them to serve until the expiration of the ADSC. For example, a graduate of the Reserve Officer Training Corps incurs

---

[28] Air Force personnel data for August 2016 provided to RAND by the Air Force Personnel Center.

an ADSC of four years, while Undergraduate Pilot Training (UPT) obligates an officer to serve for ten years after graduation from UPT (AFI 36-2107). Officers' continued service beyond the expiration of an ADSC is not obligatory, and they are then free to separate if they choose.

While reenlistment relates exclusively to enlisted service members, the main measure of retention among officers is survival, or CCRs. CCRs are most commonly depicted graphically. Beginning at 100 percent, they trace the decreasing proportion of officers of a given accessions cohort remaining on active duty at each year of service. The Defense Officer Personnel Management Act stipulates an "up or out" promotion system wherein each rank has a maximum allowable number of years of service that, if not met, require an officer to separate. Promotion to O-2 and O-3 is based on an officer being "fully qualified," but subsequent promotions depend on an officer being "best and fully qualified" (Military Leadership Diversity Commission, 2011). Thus, retention past O-3 is complicated by an officer's promotion success, whereas below O-3, retention is a more a function of ADSC and service proclivity.

In addition to the fact that male and female officers tend to differ on key characteristics that relate to promotion, persistent differences in retention are an important driver of overall differences in patterns of military career progression (Asch, Miller, and Malchiodi, 2012; Hosek et al., 2001). These differences tend to be largest at early retention points in a military officer's career. In a study of officers across all military services, Asch, Miller, and Malchiodi (2012) find that female officers generally have lower retention rates than white men, conditional on a number of factors.[29] In particular, female officers generally have lower retention at O-3 and O-5. The one exception is black women, who have higher retention rates at O-3 than white men. Focusing on Air Force officers, Lim et al. (2014) note that the largest gender gap in retention is between the fifth and seventh years of service, after which the gap narrows.

Explaining the Gender Gap in Retention

Two recent studies have attempted to explain the gender gap in officer retention based on observed characteristics. For example, Asch, Miller, and Weinberger (2016) found that gender differences in such characteristics as occupational group and family status, including marital status and the presence of children, were important in explaining gender differences in retention at certain career points. However, they found that these and other observable characteristics were not able to fully explain the gender gap in retention. Lim and colleagues (2014) similarly attempted to isolate the causes underlying the differences in military retention between male and female Air Force officers. By controlling for marital status, race/ethnicity, children, rank, occupation, and source of commission, a population of male officers with similar attributes to female officers was created as a comparison. The authors found that, among young officers, gender retention differences can be partially explained by demographic and career

---

[29] Asch, Miller, and Malchiodi (2012) adjust for differences in service, source of commission, prior enlisted service, a general occupation grouping, deployment experience, marital status, and education.

characteristics. However, as an officer becomes more senior, the explanatory strength of these traits diminishes.

Other prior research examining gender differences in female officer retention has taken a similar qualitative approach as this study, although the work was not focused on the Air Force specifically. For example, based on a series of focus groups with military officers across the service components, previous research by Hosek et al. (2001) attributes higher rates of female separation to three broad influences. The first of these influences was that women tended to concentrate in career fields with fewer long-term promotion opportunities, which lead some women to separate before the risk of a failed promotion is realized. Second, women expressed a weariness of having to fight harder than their male peers for recognition and acceptance as capable members of their profession. Third, female military members were far more likely to have an employed spouse than their male peers and typically carried a larger share of the burden of maintaining a home and raising children. The authors concluded that, in light of these factors, many women believed the costs of military service outweigh its benefits, although the vast majority of those separating expressed pride in their service and regretted feeling obligated to separate.

The difficulties of balancing motherhood with demanding work schedules have been discussed in other work on female retention in the military as well. For example, Mady Wechsler Segal (1986), who has written extensively on gender and diversity within the military, builds on previous work by Coser (1974) by describing both the military and the family as "greedy institutions" that "make great demands of individuals in terms of commitment, loyalty, time and energy of their members" (Segal, 1986, p. 9).[30] Women are seen as having a "conflict of allegiance" between family demands and occupational requirements, and Segal asserts that although the conflict also exists for men, it is generally greater for women. In another study, Bourg and Segal state, "When individuals experience conflict or competition between work and family, most would prefer to settle the conflict in favor of the family, potentially resulting in decreased commitment to the work organization" (1999, p. 636). Looking at the Army specifically, they suggest that supportive policies from the Army that seek to mitigate the work-family conflict are effective because "resources expended in convincing soldiers that the Army cares for their family increases soldiers' commitment" (Bourg and Segal, 1999, p. 649).

The well-being of military families, including military divorce, may also contribute to female retention. Under the assumption that satisfying relationships with their spouses and children increase effectiveness, the military has made extensive efforts to support military families. In support of military families, quality of life services such as child care and health care offered to service members are generally superior to any related programs in the private sector (Karney and Crown, 2007). However, demand for subsidized DoD CDCs often exceeds available spaces,

---

[30] Other works on gender, diversity and the military include Segal and Segal (1983); Segal et al. (1998); Rohall, Segal, and Segal, (1999); Cooney et al. (2003); and Segal, Thanner, and Segal (2007).

which can transform this quality of life benefit into a source of frustration for military families. Further, child care center schedules do not always align with the work schedules of parents who may have to work 24-hour operations (Military Compensation and Retirement Modernization Commission, 2015). This concern may be particularly burdensome for female service members whose spouses are more likely to be employed.

Additionally, a unique concern for dual-military couples is maintaining geographic proximity to their spouse. Considering that a much higher percentage of female service members are married to male service members than the opposite (DoD, 2015a), joint-spouse location concerns are more common among women. While a program was enacted to minimize the hardships of dual military couples, it can be increasingly difficult with each assignment cycle for both spouses to be assigned to a new job in a career-enhancing assignment. Frequently, one spouse will receive an assignment that is more favorable to his or her career progression, after which each assignment cycle snowballs with the result that one spouse holds the "dominant career." If the man holds the dominant career, it is more likely that the women will separate given their perceived reduced benefits from a stagnated career path. Also of note is that women in dual military couples, when faced with a hypothetical long separation, tend to state that they are more likely to separate than their spouse, and more married women than married men considered their career as subordinate to that of their spouse (Hosek et al., 2001).

Using previously collected military survey data, the Military Leadership Diversity Commission (2011) examined differences in service members' attitudes toward military life to try to better understand the gender gap in retention. They found that female officers across the service components were as likely as male officers to be satisfied with military life and report that they intended to remain in the service. However, they were less likely than male officers to report that they saw the military as a career. In terms of reasons for separating from the military, the Commission found that both men and women cited dissatisfaction with their job, low pay, and lack of advancement opportunities. For female officers, they also cited high frequency of deployments and a desire to settle in one location as key reasons for separating.

Starting at a much earlier point in a military officer's career, a study conducted at the U.S. Naval Academy (Smith and Rosenstein, 2017) utilized survey data to understand how career attitudes and intentions develop and are influenced during the early stages of women's and men's socialization at the Academy. Motivated by a desire to understand why retention rates of women lag behind men, they initially expected that a range of factors—such as professional role models, familial influences, and social influences— would positively influence first-year students' intentions to stay in the military. Instead they found weak correlative relationships overall between such factors and years of intended service at that early stage of officers' careers.

Thus, prior research has found several potential factors important in accounting for gender differences in military officer retention, with these often related to family issues. However, this research does not fully explain the gender gap.

Some Civilian Retention Issues May Be Comparable to Military Retention Issues

While the intricacies of military employment are in some ways incomparable to employment in the civilian sector, research findings on retention in the civilian sector may still offer insight or highlight other avenues to explore when examining military retention. For example, a recent meta-analysis examining predictors of turnover found that key predictors include job attitudes, such as job satisfaction and organizational commitment, along with other characteristics of the work environment, including job content, stress, work group cohesion, and leadership (Griffeth, Hom, and Gaertner, 2000). These factors are likely similarly important in the military context.

Research on retention improvement initiatives in academic and corporate environments may also provide additional insight into issues important for retaining female service members. For example, a number of studies have examined workplace policies on influencing retention both in the civilian labor force and among first-generation college students. A study of human resources practices and their influence on employee turnover found that flexibility and support were both important to reducing turnover, and that each affected men and women differently (Batt and Valcour, 2003). According to this study, women generally favor more-supportive supervisors while men favor flexible scheduling. Other research has found that, although both genders benefit from mentorship, women are more likely than men to state that mentors played a role in their success (Gibbons and Woodside, 2014). This emphasizes the importance of the finding that men may avoid mentoring women, fearing perceptions of favoritism or vulnerability to accusations of sexual harassment (Hosek et al., 2001).

A 2008 Harvard Business Review research report investigated the high levels of attrition of midcareer women in science, engineering, and technology workforces (Hewlett et al., 2008). While the findings of this report do not specifically relate to female military attrition, the stressors of a demanding career on the cutting edge of these professions may be comparable to the stress imposed by a military lifestyle. The factors identified by this report were broadly categorized into the following cultures: hostile macho cultures, isolation, mysterious career paths, systems of risk and reward, and extreme work pressures. Hostile macho cultures were defined as unsupportive workplaces in which women are constantly forced to prove themselves, and the corporate culture implicitly favors married men with the ability to work late knowing their children will be cared for. Isolation occurs in environments with relatively few women and the existence of an "old boys' network." Mysterious career paths are symptomatic of fewer mentors and sponsors for midcareer female professionals. The system of risks and rewards speaks to the bias of rewarding individuals able to drop everything else to avert a catastrophe. Women, particularly those without a strong support network, are less likely to engage in such high-risk maneuvers, generally have more constraints making them less able to meet the demands therein, and finally often are more focused on averting disasters preventatively—a task that is necessary but less commonly rewarded. Finally, extreme work pressures involved with frequent travel and varied and lengthy work hours are generally more taxing on women, who generally have greater family and household requirements (Hewlett et al., 2008).

Hewlett et al. discuss a number of corporate initiatives designed to combat these negative pressures. By increasing the numbers of women through targeted recruiting, many companies hope to reach the critical mass necessary to overcome the effects of isolation. Other companies encourage their talented women to remain in technical line duties, which are more often tied to promotion opportunities in order to improve the diversity of senior leadership. Some corporations are expanding and lengthening their maternity leave and leave-of-absence programs, acknowledging that family demands may force the separation of some individuals who would rather continue to serve again in the future. Through a wide array of corporate policies and programs, there is significant interest in improving the ability of women to complete longer, more satisfying, and productive careers (Hewlett et al., 2008).

Another body of civilian literature focuses on the career strategies of both men and women. One study examined when men and women may scale back their work effort and determined that women tend to scale back on their jobs at the birth of their first child, while men more commonly scale back at other life events or when their careers "stabilize" (Becker and Moen, 1999). Women in this study also stressed that a greater ability to maintain a family and work flexibility was crucial for their continued workforce presence. A study examining the U.S. and European labor markets highlighted how such incentives shape behavior, finding differences in policies that were then associated with differences in outcomes for women. In Europe, women are given more paid maternity leave than women in the United States and subsequently have a greater ability to switch to part-time work without fear of losing their jobs (Blau and Kahn, 2013). Blau and Kahn (2013) concluded that, while Europe experiences greater female participation in the labor force partly because of the increased flexibility offered during and following maternity leave, fewer European women rise to senior positions compared with those in the United States, where greater commitment may be implicitly demanded of women who elect to remain in the labor force.

Literature relating to civilian family concerns is also significant, because the requirements of many nonmilitary jobs influence employees' relationships with their families. In an analysis of how child care responsibilities affected employment stability and turnover, Hofferth and Collins (2000) linked increased availability and flexibility of nonparental child care with higher female retention. Studying civilian geographic relocations both with and separated from one's family, Shaffer and colleagues (2001) concluded that retention following geographic relocation is strongly related to the success of the family in the new environment and perceived work-family conflict. Yet the effect of work-family conflict and mitigating effects of work-family initiatives may depend significantly on the specific employer or profession, making extrapolation of civilian literature to military retention difficult. For instance, one concern that has been raised is that retention is frequently measured by self-reported employee turnover *intentions* instead of experimental or quasi-experimental studies using actual turnover (Kelly et al., 2008). Thus, while some comparisons may be drawn between civilian job turnover and military retention, drawing firm conclusions may first require addressing such concerns or should perhaps be limited to general topics such as work-life balance.

Summary

Officers incur a duty commitment upon commissioning, as they do for some training (e.g., pilot training). Once an officer completes his or her obligatory service commitment, he or she is free to leave the service. However, when it comes to female separations, some differences emerge. Prior research has found that women separate at higher rates than men. Research has not fully explained these differences, although some factors may include women tending to concentrate in fields with fewer long-term promotion opportunities, feelings that they have to work harder to receive the same respect as their male peers, and a higher likelihood of having an employed spouse than their male peers. Other research suggests that family reasons are a primary motivation. For married couples with both members in the military, finding colocated assignments can place a strain on marriages, with such assignment becoming more difficult as the couple advances in rank and seniority.

Some civilian retention issues may be comparable to those found in the military. Career flexibility and supportive supervisors have been cited as important influences, especially for women. Other research cites hostile cultures favoring male attitudes, ambiguous information about career paths (symptomatic of a lack of mentors), systems of risk and reward, and extreme work pressures. Still other research found that women highly prize work flexibility. However, comparisons between the civilian and military workplaces should be regarded with caution and perhaps limited to more general topics.

Appendix B. Base Selection Methodology

To ensure that focus groups included a broad and representative sample of female Air Force officers, we carefully deliberated over the choice of bases to visit. Budget constraints necessitated some trade-offs. However, deliberate sampling ensured that focus groups were conducted at bases containing a diverse mission set and sufficient female representation to support multiple focus groups. This appendix describes our process for selecting the bases included in the study.

First, retention patterns show that female officers have lower continuation rates than male officers, with the majority of female officers separating from active duty service by seven years for nonrated occupations and by 11 years for rated occupations, which often have a longer initial service commitment. For example, most Air Force officer occupations require a four-year active duty service commitment. However, pilots make a ten-year active duty service commitment, and both Combat System Officers and Air Battle Managers make a six-year active duty service commitment. Therefore, in consultation with the study sponsors, we chose to target female officers who had 1–12 years of service. This would allow us to talk with female officers who would most likely be in key career decisions points for retention.

Through discussions with the study sponsor, we then identified additional criteria for selecting the Air Force bases included in our study. These included trying to get representation across MAJCOMs, various functional concentrations (i.e., career fields), and geographic locations. In terms of geographic diversity, we focused on trying to get some geographic dispersion across the continental United States (CONUS) as well as the type of surrounding community as either rural or urban. It was beyond the scope of this study to visit any Air Force bases that were outside of the continental United States (OCONUS).[31] Finally, we looked at having a mix of types of bases, including whether a base was joint and the presence of a guard or reserve unit. Using these criteria, we then examined which bases would also have a sufficient number of female officers with which to conduct focus groups in our target range of 1–12 years of service using the AFPC's IDEAS.[32]

In consultation with the study sponsors, we selected the 12 Air Force installations presented in Table B.1. The table also provides an overview of the base location, MAJCOM association,

---

[31] This precluded our ability to reach the two geographic MAJCOMs—Pacific Air Forces and U.S. Air Forces in Europe–Air Forces Africa.

[32] We tried to target bases that had at least 100 female officers in our target range for years of service, knowing that only a small sample at each installation would likely be interested and available for participation in our focus groups. This helped us ensure that we would have sufficient numbers with which to conduct our groups given the available project funds. In some cases, however, ensuring that we had sufficient representation across Air Force specialties took priority, and we had lower numbers of female officers from which to draw.

whether the base is joint, and the presence of a guard or reserve unit in the area. We also show the geographic distribution of the selected bases in Figure B.1.

Table B.1. Final Base Selection

Base	State	MAJCOM	Joint	Guard	Reserve
Andrews	Washington, D.C.	Headquarters	Y	Y	Y
Barksdale	Louisiana	Global Strike Command			Y
F.E. Warren	Wyoming	Global Strike Command		Y	
Hurlburt	Florida	Special Operations Command			
Lackland	Texas	Air Education and Training Command	Y	Y	Y
Langley	Virginia	Air Combat Command	Y	Y	
Los Angeles	California	Space Command			
McChord	Washington	Air Mobility Command	Y		Y
Randolph	Texas	Air Education and Training Command	Y		Y
Schriever	Colorado	Space Command			Y
Seymour Johnson	North Carolina	Air Combat Command			Y
Wright-Patterson	Ohio	Materiel Command			Y

Figure B.1. Air Force Bases Included in Focus Group Sample

Major Active-Duty Air Force Installations

Limitations

There are a few limitations worth noting with regard to our base selection. First, the decision to focus on bases with larger numbers of female officers in our target years of service inevitably biases us toward larger bases. Further, these larger bases are less likely to be located in rural areas because a large base population rarely remains especially rural. We attempted to compensate for this by ensuring our focus groups intentionally asked participants to consider their experiences at prior, smaller bases.

In addition, the decision not to sample officers with more than 12 years of service limited our ability to investigate retention decisions that occur further along officers' careers, including immediately before and following retirement eligibility for those who elect to continue beyond 20 years of service. Finally, the decision to sample solely CONUS bases restricts the geographic diversity of participants and makes location impacts on retention decisions more difficult to discern. It could be that a PCS from CONUS to OCONUS is undesirable and pushes individuals to separate. Alternatively, they could return stateside reinvigorated by an assignment perceived as "on the front lines" and eager to continue their service domestically.

Appendix C. Focus Group Protocols

Focus Group Protocol: Female Officers at Critical Decision Points in Their Careers and Female Officers with Separation Dates

Provide Study Overview and Administer Consent

General Background Questions

1. We are first going to begin with questions regarding the characteristics of this group.

    A. What is your current pay grade?

    B. What is your career field?

    C. What was your commissioning source?

    D. How many years of service have you provided since commissioning?

    E. How many months or years do you have remaining on your current service obligation?

    F. Do you currently intend to remain in the Air Force for at least 20 years?

        i.   For those who do not intend to remain in the Air Force:

            a. Do you have a separation date?

            b. Are you planning to remain affiliated with the Air Force by serving in the Guard/Reserves?

Career Choices

2. Why/how did you choose your career field?

    A. When deciding, did you consider the civilian transferability of the career field?

3. To what extent do you or did you consider senior leadership to be one of your career goals? Why?

4. How would you describe the quality and amount of feedback you received about your career options and career potential in the Air Force?

Retention Factors

We are interested in hearing about your own personal thoughts with regard to your career as well as what you know regarding reasons your fellow peers have chosen to stay or leave.

5. In general, what factors do you think contribute to female officers leaving the Air Force earlier in their careers than male officers?

6. How do personal matters or family influence female officers' decisions regarding how long to stay in the Air Force?

    A. *Probes:*

        i. For female officers' with spouses or partners, how do spouses/partners influence female officer decisions regarding staying in or leaving the Air Force? How, if at all, does compatibility of their career with their spouse's career play a factor?

        ii. How do children influence female officer decisions regarding staying in or leaving the Air Force?

        iii. How does number of deployments/PCS influence female officer decisions regarding staying in or leaving the Air Force?

    B. How might the Air Force better assist female officers with family-related matters?

        i. How do you think the extension of the maternity leave policy to 12 weeks may influence female officer retention?

        ii. Are you aware of the Air Force Career Intermission Program?[33] If so, how do you think this program might influence decisions to stay in or leave the Air Force?

---

[33] The program allows regular Air Force and career status Active Guard or Reserve officers and enlisted members to be inactivated and transferred to the Individual Ready Reserve, receiving partial pay for up to three years, before returning to active duty. The intent is that individuals won't have to separate to take care of personal or other professional concerns.

7. How do elements of their Air Force career and work environment influence female officers' decisions regarding how long to stay in the Air Force?

   A. *Probes:*

      i.   How, if at all, does leadership, such as immediate leadership or leadership at unit level, influence female officer decisions regarding staying in or leaving the Air Force?

      ii. Are there characteristics of your career field that may contribute to female officers deciding to leave the Air Force? If so, what are these?

      iii. How, if at all, do you think the gender composition of a unit influences female officer experiences and decisions regarding staying in or leaving the Air Force?

   B. How might the Air Force better assist female officers with these career and work environment elements?

      i.   What changes to or additional Air Force benefits, programs, or policies would lead female officers to further consider *remaining* in the Air Force beyond their obligation?

8. Who have you (or would you) talk with about deciding whether to stay in or leave the Air Force (e.g., spouse, friends, other Airmen)? How have they influenced your decision?

Closing Question

Do you have any additional suggestions for changes that can be made that could improve the Air Force's ability to retain female officers in the Air Force or to improve the career and working environment more generally?

Focus Group Protocol: Female Officers Who Have Already Separated from Active Duty and are Now in Guard/Reserves

Provide Study Overview and Administer Consent

General Background Questions

1. We are first going to begin with questions regarding the characteristics of this group.

    A. Which are you currently affiliated with: the Air Force Guard or the Air Force Reserves?

    B. What was your active duty commissioning source?

    C. How many years of active duty service did you provide after commissioning?

    D. After approximately how many years in the active duty Air Force did you decide you wanted to leave active duty?

    E. What was the approximate date on which you separated from the active duty Air Force?

        i. On what date did you join the Air Force Guard/Reserves?

    F. What was your pay grade when leaving the active duty Air Force?

        i. What is your current pay grade?

    G. What was your career field when leaving the active duty Air Force?

        i. What is your current career field?

Career Choices

We are now going to ask you several questions regarding your career. These questions focus on aspects of your active duty career.

2. Why/how did you choose your active duty career field?

    A. When deciding your active duty career field, did you consider the civilian transferability of the career field?

3. To what extent did you consider senior leadership for your active duty career? Why?

4. How would you describe the quality and amount of feedback you received about your career options and career potential in the active duty Air Force?

Retention Factors

5. In general, what are some of the factors that contributed to your decision to leave the active duty Air Force?

6. How did personal matters or family influence your decision regarding leaving the active duty Air Force?

   A. *Probes:*

      i. If you have a spouse or partner, how did your spouse/partner influence your decision to leave the active duty Air Force? How, if at all, did compatibility of your career with your spouse's or partner's career play a factor?

      ii. If you have children, how did they influence your decision to leave the active duty Air Force?

      iii. How did number of deployments/PCS influence your decision to leave the active duty Air Force?

   B. How might the active duty Air Force have better assisted you with family-related matters?

      i. How would the extension of the maternity leave policy to 12 weeks have influenced your decision?

      ii. Are you aware of the Air Force Career Intermission Program?[34] If so, did you consider participating in this program while in the active duty Air Force?

7. How did elements of your active duty Air Force career and work environment influence your decision regarding leaving the active duty Air Force?

   A. *Probes:*

      i. How, if at all, did leadership, such as immediate leadership or leadership at unit level, influence your decision to leave the active duty Air Force?

      ii. How, if at all, did the gender composition of your units influence your decision to leave the active duty Air Force?

      iii. How might the Air Force have better assisted you with these career and work environment elements?

---

[34] The program allows regular Air Force and career status Active Guard or Reserve officers and enlisted members to be inactivated and transferred to the Individual Ready Reserve, receiving partial pay for up to three years, before returning to active duty. The intent is that individuals won't have to separate to take care of personal or other professional concerns.

B. *Probes:*

    i.   What are some of the Air Force policies or programs that led you to decide to leave the active duty Air Force?

    ii.   What changes to or additional Air Force benefits, programs, or policies would have led you to further consider *remaining* in the active duty Air Force?

8. Who did you talk with about deciding whether to stay in or leave the active duty Air Force (e.g., spouse, friends, other Airmen)? How did they influence your decision?

9. What made you decide to remain affiliated with the Air Force by serving in the Guard/Reserves?

Closing Question

Do you have any additional suggestions for changes that can be made that could have improved the Air Force's ability to retain you in the Air Force or to improve the career and working environment more generally?

Appendix D. Qualitative Coding Approach and Coding Guide for Female Air Force Officer Retention Focus Groups

Once we completed all focus groups, we uploaded the detailed focus group transcripts into NVivo, a qualitative data analysis software program. RAND researchers then coded transcripts from the focus group notes to identify key themes common across the groups. We used an integrated approach of deductive and inductive coding, with the protocol questions guiding the initial development of codes. We then added additional themes that emerged within these broader codes throughout the coding process. We also coded focus group comments according to participants' background characteristics obtained during the sessions so we could identify any unique trends for different pay grades or career fields, for example.

The content coding was divided between two members of the research team. To ensure coder consistency, these two researchers both separately coded, or double-coded, one set of focus groups notes, then ran a coding comparison and discussed any discrepancies. The researchers repeated this process with another set of focus group notes, and, satisfied with the coder consistency, began coding individually. To ensure acceptable levels of coder consistency remained, the researchers conducted coding comparisons at additional points throughout the process, double-coding seven sets of focus groups notes in total. For each double-coded set of focus group notes, the research team conducted interrater reliability tests, measured by the Cohen's Kappa coefficient and percent agreement at each coding node.[35] We conducted these tests for all nodes and then just for content notes, excluding the nodes for participants' background characteristics, as these were coded previously by another team member. Table D.1 provides the average Kappa coefficient and percent agreement for all nodes and just content nodes by focus groups we tested. Because levels of consistency remained favorable, the researchers determined that additional double-coding and assessment was not necessary beyond these seven focus groups.

---

[35] Cohen's Kappa coefficient (Cohen, 1960) is a statistical measure of interrater reliability that aims to account for coding agreement occurring by chance. Guidelines recommended for interpreting Kappa values are as follows: less than 0.40, poor agreement; 0.40–0.75, fair to good agreement; more than 0.75, excellent agreement.

Table D.1. Interrater Reliability Test Results

Focus Group	All Nodes		Content Nodes Only	
	Average Kappa	Average % Agreement	Average Kappa	Average % Agreement
1	0.79	98.00	0.64	96.50
2	0.85	98.79	0.74	97.94
3	0.84	98.68	0.73	97.78
4	0.89	98.67	0.81	97.78
5	0.86	97.99	0.76	96.58
6	0.83	98.66	0.71	97.71
7	0.88	98.41	0.79	97.29

Coding Guide Instructions

Participant Characteristic Codes

To capture background characteristics of focus group participants, coders will first code all text by participant rank and career field group as well as appropriately code all text for those participants who are in the Reserve Component (RC) or have a separation date. Every participant will be coded for rank and career field group but only those participants in the RC or with a separation date will be coded to indicate those two characteristics. Focus group notes will include designations for these participant characteristic codes in brackets following the number assigned to the participant throughout the notes. Code all text spoken by each participant according to the designated characteristic codes. Level 1 codes are the broadest, with Level 2 and Level 3 codes becoming increasingly specific. Coders should code at the most specific level of code possible and not code the associated broader code levels. The participant characteristic codes are as follows:

Level 1	Level 2	Level 3	Description	Corresponding Protocol Question
Rank			Participant rank/pay grade (do not code level 1)	"What is your current pay grade?"
	O-1		O-1 (second lieutenant)	
	O-2		O-2 (first lieutenant)	
	O-3		O-3 (captain)	
	O-4+		O-4 (major) and O5 (lieutenant colonel)	
Career field group			Participant AFSC or career field reduced to major subgroup (with the exception of pilot) (do not code Level 1)	"What is your career field?"
	Operations		Operations includes Navigator, Combat Systems Officer, Air Battle Manager, Combat Rescue Officer, Special Tactics Officer, Space, Missiles, Intel, Cyber, Remotely Piloted Aircraft	
		Pilot	Pilots are also part of Operations, but we will code them separately as a subcode to Operations. Only code pilots as Level 3 and not as Level 2	
	Logistics		Logistics includes Maintenance, Logistics	
	Support		Support includes Security Forces, Civil Engineer, Public Affairs, Personnel, Support	
	Medical		Medical includes Doctors, Dentists, Nurses, Social Workers, Flight Surgeons, etc.	
	Professional		Professional includes Judge Advocate General, Chaplain	
	Acquisitions		Acquisitions includes Scientists, Engineers (except Civil), Contracting, Finance, Acquisition	
	Special investigations		Special Investigations includes Office of Special Investigations	
	Special duty		Special Duty	
RC			Currently a member of the Air Force Reserves or Air National Guard	If RC member is in AC group, no corresponding protocol question. RC information emerges from background questions. If group is composed of all RC members, this should be indicated at the top of the focus group notes
Separation date			Participant indicates she has a separation date to leave the active duty Air Force	"Do you have a separation date?" Or participant may indicate a separate date when answering "How many months or years do you have remaining on your current service obligation?"
For discussion			Information is unclear and needs to be flagged to review with team and recoded once clarified	N/A

Content Codes

Once coders have coded all focus group notes to capture participant characteristics, we will code the discussion text for content and themes. This coding will not focus on the individual participant level, but the discussion content in general. Code all text that addresses the topics as defined. Make sure coded text captures enough of the discussion to provide necessary context for comments made. Corresponding protocol questions are provided for reference, but coder should code text on each theme throughout the notes, not just in response to the corresponding protocol question. In many instances, a question may not specifically be asked because the theme emerged organically in the discussion.

Level 1 codes are the broadest codes, with Levels 2, 3, 4, and 5 becoming increasingly specific. Coders should code at the most specific level of code possible and do not need to code the associated broader code levels. Code as many content codes as are relevant to the comment. For example, a comment about a mil-to-mil marriage being difficult because of child care issues and deployments should be coded as: Mil-mil, child, and deploy.

Level 1	Level 2	Level 3	Level 4	Level 5	Description	Corresponding Protocol Question
Background					Additional background questions of interest not captured in participant characteristics; code background on number of years served and number of years remaining at Level 1	
	Remain 20 years				Participants' intention of remaining in the Air Force for at least 20 years; only code in response to this question	"Do you currently intend to remain in the Air Force for at least 20 years?"
	Remain in RC				Whether participants are planning to remain affiliated with the Reserves or Guard if they leave active duty Air Force	"Are you planning to remain affiliated with the Air Force by serving in the Guard/Reserves"
Career choices					Discussion of participant career choices and related comments (do not code level 1)	
	Why/how chose				Why or how participants chose their current career field, including why they joined the Air Force	"Why/how did you choose your career field?"
		Civilian transfer			Consideration of civilian transferability of Air Force career field	"When deciding [on your career field choice], did you consider the civilian transferability of the career field?"
	Senior leadership				Participant comments regarding their personal goals for senior leadership or lack thereof; do not code for comments on feedback they receive regarding command potential	"To what extent do you or did you consider senior leadership to be one of your career goals?"
	Career feedback				Comments regarding feedback received on career choice and AF career path in general. Includes pre- and post-commissioning feedback as well as formal and informal feedback. May also include discussion about guidance provided by mentors in addition to chain of command.	"How would you describe the quality and amount of feedback you received about your career options and career potential in the Air Force?"

Level 1	Level 2	Level 3	Level 4	Level 5	Description	Corresponding Protocol Question
Retention factors					Factors that influence female retention. These should include comments about factors that affect retention negatively and positively. Also should include comments stated that a certain factor does not influence retention. (do not code at Level 1)	Question 5 applies to all subcodes below
	Family/personal life				Retention factors related to family and/or personal lives	Questions 6, 6ai, 6aii, 6aiii apply to all subcodes below
		Spouse			Spouse issues (e.g., spouse's career, marriage, divorce); do not code if talking about dating or finding someone to marry, that should go under the "other" code	
			Military-to-military		Issues related to female officers being married to another active duty military member (e.g., co-location challenges, deployment, BAH pay)	
				BAH*	Issues related to proposed removal of BAH for one member of a joint couple	
			Civilian		Issues related to female officers married to civilian spouses (e.g., stay-at-home dad enables Air Force career because providing child care, spouse's civilian career suffers due to frequent PCS)	
				Spouse programs	Issues related to military spouse programs or groups	
		Children			Issues related to children (e.g., CDC issues, separation issues), including wanting children or thinking about how having children may affect later retention	
			Child care*		Issues related to child care, including CDCs	
			Family Care Plan*		Issues related to Air Force Family Care plan	
			Hours/ schedule*		Issues related to work hours and schedule and effect on children or time with children	
			School*		Issues related to children's school	

Level 1	Level 2	Level 3	Level 4	Level 5	Description	Corresponding Protocol Question
Retention factors (cont.)		Pregnancy			Issues related to being pregnant or timing of pregnancy (e.g., work limitations due to pregnancy or waiting to get pregnant because of deployments)	
			Birthing medical options*		Issues related to options for giving birth (e.g., hospital choice, midwife) with TRICARE	
			Breastfeeding*		Issues related to breastfeeding after pregnancy	
			Miscarriage*		Issues related to experiences with miscarriage	
			Discrimination*		Issues related to pregnancy discrimination experienced in the Air Force	
		Deployment			Issues related to number of or frequency of deployments on family/personal life (*will often be double-coded with above codes)	
			Positive— Deployment*		Positive comments about deployments	
		PCS			Issues related to number of or frequency of PCS on family/personal life (*will often be double-coded with above codes)	
			Positive-PCS*		Positive comments about PCS	
		Location			Issues related to the desirability of a specific location and impact on family/personal life (*will often be double-coded with above codes)	
		Other (family/ personal)			Other factors influencing female officer retention related to family or personal lives not captured in family/personal life subcodes above	
			Benefits*		Issues related to Air Force benefits (e.g., health care) and effect on family or personal life	
			Dating*		Issues related to dating in the Air Force and being a single female Airman	
			Female health care*		Issues specific to female health care (e.g., gynecological issues)	
			Work-family balance*		Issues related to work-family balance and Air Force careers	

Level 1	Level 2	Level 3	Level 4	Level 5	Description	Corresponding Protocol Question
Retention factors (cont.)			PME*		Issues related to PME that affect family or personal life	
			Support network*		Issues related to support network for family or personal lives	
	Career/work environment		TDY*		Effect of being sent TDY on family or personal life	
					Retention factors related to career or work environment	Questions 7, 7ai, 7aii apply to all subcodes below
		Leadership			Ways leadership influence female retention	
			Female leaders*		Importance of having female leaders and role models and how they influence female officer retention	
			Mentoring*		Influence and importance of having mentorship from above	
		AFSC-specific			Characteristics of a career field that may affect retention decisions (*may often be double-coded with gender composition if referencing a specific career field)	
		Gender composition			Impact of the gender composition of a unit or career field on female retention (e.g., being treated differently for being a woman—including treatment by female civilian spouses—and having other women to talk with	
		Other			Other factors influencing female officer retention related to career or work environment not captured above	
			Flexible career paths*		Discussion of desire for flexible or alternative career paths and effect on retention	
			Civilian opportunities*		Effect of civilian employment opportunities on retention	
			Cross-train*		Comments related to opportunities to cross-train into another career field	
			Long hours or shift work*		Effect of long hours or shift work on retention (not connected to impact on family)	

Level 1	Level 2	Level 3	Level 4	Level 5	Description	Corresponding Protocol Question
Retention factors (cont.)			Sexual assault/harassment*		Experiences with or fears of sexual assault or harassment and impact on retention	
			Benefits*		Effect of benefits (e.g., salary, retirement, education) on retention (not connected to impact on family)	
			RIF*		Effect of force reduction or force shaping on retention	
	Biggest impact				Factors noted to be the No. 1 influencer of female retention or "deal breakers." This code should be coded in addition to the content of what that factor is (e.g., "co-location for a mil-to-mil marriage is the number one reason I would get out of the Air Force" should be coded as Mil-mil and Biggest Impact).	Comments about the most important or biggest factor may be made throughout the discussion and can be captured through this code. This code can also capture any wrap-up questions that ask for No. 1 factors or deal breakers.
Air Force improvements					Ways the Air Force can better assist female officers to address retention factors (e.g., policies, programs). What can the Air Force do to improve female retention? (code all suggested improvements at this node that are not related to maternity leave or career intermission); should be coded in addition to the content of retention factor the improvement would address	
	Maternity leave				Extension of the maternity leave policy to 12 weeks (also includes comments about extension of time for fitness testing or deployment allowed after birth of a child); do not need to double-code with pregnancy or children if brought up as part of the discussion of the extension of maternity leave	"How do you think the extension of the maternity leave policy to 12 weeks may influence female officer retention?"
	Career intermission				Comments related to awareness of and impact on retention of CIP; do not need to double-code with other factors if brought up as part of the discussion on the career intermission program	"Are you aware of the Air Force Career Intermission Program? If so, how do you think this program might influence decisions to stay in or leave the Air Force?"

78

Level 1	Level 2	Level 3	Level 4	Level 5	Description	Corresponding Protocol Question
Who talk with					Who do participants discuss retention decisions with?	Question 9 "Who have you (or would you) talk with about deciding whether to stay in or leave the Air Force (e.g., spouse, friends, other Airmen)? How have they influenced your decision?" Note: this question was not asked for many of the groups
For discussion					Flag comments that need review by team and coding assignment is unclear. This text can be pulled up and reviewed and recoded after team discussion and clarification.	
Quote					Flag comments that could be used in briefing and report to illustrate key theme	

*Codes added for additional depth of analysis after conducting initial coding process.

References

AFI—*See* Air Force Instruction.

AFPC—*See* Air Force Personnel Center.

Air Force Guidance Memorandum, *Medical Care Management,* AFGM to AFI 44-102, January 6, 2017. As of March 8, 2017:
http://static.e-publishing.af.mil/production/1/af_sg/publication/afi44-102/afi44-102.pdf

Air Force Instruction 36-2107, *Active Duty Service Commitments*, November 25, 2009.

Air Force Instruction 36-2640, *Executing Total Force Development*, December 16, 2008.

Air Force Instruction 36-3003, *Military Leave Program,* May 11, 2016.

Air Force Instruction 44-102, *Medical Community Health Management*, November 17, 1999.

Air Force Personnel Center, *2011-2012 Active Duty/AGR Retention Survey Results*, 2013.

———, Interactive Demographic Analysis System, officer extract data, August 2016.

Air Force Sergeants Association Division 4, "Air Force Benefits Fact Sheet," January 3, 2017. As of July 20, 2017:
http://afsadiv4.org/wp-content/uploads/2016/03/2017-AF-Benefits-Fact-Sheet-3-Jan-17.pdf

Asch, Beth J., Trey Miller, and Alessandro Malchiodi, *A New Look at Gender and Minority Differences in Officer Career Progression in the Military*, Santa Monica, Calif.: RAND Corporation, TR-1159-OSD, 2012. As of July 19, 2017:
https://www.rand.org/pubs/technical_reports/TR1159.html

Asch, Beth J., Trey Miller, and Gabriel Weinberger, *Can We Explain Gender Differences in Officer Career Progression?* Santa Monica, Calif.: RAND Corporation, RR-1288-OSD, 2016. As of July 19, 2017:
https://www.rand.org/pubs/research_reports/RR1288.html

Batt, Rosemary, and P. Monique Valcour, "Human Resources Practices as Predictors of Work-Family Outcomes and Employee Turnover," *Industrial Relations: A Journal of Economy and Society,* Vol. 42, No. 2, 2003, pp. 189–220.

Becker, Penny Edgell, and Phyllis Moen, "Scaling Back: Dual-Earner Couples Work-Family Strategy," *Journal of Marriage and Family,* Vol. 61, 1999, pp. 995–1007.

Blau, Francine D., and Lawrence M. Kahn, "Female Labor Supply: Why is the U.S. Falling Behind?" *American Economic Review*, Vol. 103, Papers and Proceedings of the One

Hundred Twenty-Fifth Annual Meeting of the American Economic Association, 2013, pp. 251–256.

Bourg, Chris, and Mady Wechsler Segal, "The Impact of Family Supportive Policies and Practices on Organizational Commitment to the Army," *Armed Forces & Society*, Vol. 25, No. 4, 1999, pp. 633–652.

Cohen, Jacob, "A Coefficient of Agreement for Nominal Scales," *Educational and Psychological Measurement*, Vol. 20, No.1, 1960, pp. 37–46.

Cohen, Philip N., *The Family: Diversity, Inequality, and Social Change*, New York: Norton, 2015.

Cooney, Richard T., Mady W. Segal, David R. Segal, and William W. Falk, "Racial Differences in the Impact of Military Service on the Socioeconomic Status of Women Veterans," *Armed Forces & Society,* Vol. 30, No.1, Fall 2003, pp. 53–86.

Coser, Lewis A., *Greedy Institutions: Patterns of Undivided Commitment*, New York: The Free Press, 1974.

DoD—*See* U.S. Department of Defense.

Gibbons, Melinda M., and Marianne Woodside, "Addressing the Needs of First-Generation College Students: Lessons Learned from Adults from Low-Education Families," *Journal of College Counseling*, Vol. 17, 2014, pp. 21–36.

Griffeth, Rodger W., Peter W. Hom, and Stefan Gaertner, "A Meta-Analysis of Antecedents and Correlates of Employee Turnover: Update, Moderator Tests, and Research Implications for the Next Millennium," *Journal of Management*, 2000, pp. 463–488.

Hewlett, Sylvia Ann, Carolyn Buck Luce, Lisa J. Servon, and Laura Sherbin, *The Athena Factor: Reversing the Brain Drain in Science, Engineering, and Technology*, Cambridge, Mass.: Harvard Business Review, 2008.

Hofferth, Sandra, and Nancy Collins, "Child Care and Employment Turnover," *Population Research and Policy Review*, Vol. 19, 2000, pp. 357–395.

Hosek, Susan D., Peter Tiemeyer, M. Rebecca Kilburn, Debra A. Strong, Selika Ducksworth, and Reginald Ray, *Minority and Gender Differences in Officer Career Progression*, Santa Monica, Calif.: RAND Corporation, MR-1184-OSD, 2001. As of July 19, 2017: https://www.rand.org/pubs/monograph_reports/MR1184.html

Iskra, Darlenne, Stephen Trainor, Marcia Leithauser, and Mady W. Segal, "Women's Participation in Armed Forces Cross-Nationally: Expanding Segal's Model," *Current Sociology*, Vol. 50, No. 5, 2002, 771–797.

Karney, Benjamin, and John S. Crown, *Families Under Stress: An Assessment of Data, Theory, and Research on Marriage and Divorce in the Military*, Santa Monica, Calif.: RAND Corporation, MG-599-OSD, 2007. As of July 22, 2017:
https://www.rand.org/pubs/monographs/MG599.html

Kelly, Erin L., Ellen Ernst Kossek, Leslie B. Hammer, Mary Durham, Jeremy Bray, Kelly Chermack, Lauren A. Murphy, and Dan Kaskubar, "Getting There from Here: Research on the Effects of Work-Family Initiatives on Work-Family Conflict and Business Outcomes," *Academy of Management Annals,* Vol. 2, 2008, pp. 305–349.

Lim, Nelson, Lou Mariano, Amy G. Cox, David Schulker, and Lawrence M. Hanser, *Improving Demographic Diversity in the U.S. Air Force Officer Corps*, Santa Monica, Calif.: RAND Corporation, RR-495-AF, 2014.

Lucas, J. W., and Segal, D. R., "Power, Status, and Diversity in the Military," in D. P. McDonald and K. M. Parks, eds., *Managing Diversity in the Military: The Value of Inclusion in a Culture of Uniformity*, New York: Routledge, 2012, pp. 149–161.

Military Compensation and Retirement Modernization Commission, *Final Report*, Arlington, Va., 2015.

Military Leadership Diversity Commission, *From Representation to Inclusion: Diversity Leadership for the 21st-Century,* Arlington, Va., 2011.

Olson, Pete, *2015 Active Duty Career Decisions and Military Exit Survey—Results*, Headquarters Air Force, 2016.

Public Law 110-417, Duncan Hunter National Defense Authorization Act for Fiscal Year 2009, October 14, 2008.

Public Law 113-291, Carl Levin and Howard P. "Buck" McKeon National Defense Authorization Act for Fiscal Year 2015, December 19, 2014.

Rohall, David E., Mady W. Segal, and David R. Segal, "Examining the Importance of Organizational Supports on Family Adjustment to Army Life in a Period of Increasing Separation," *Journal of Political and Military Sociology,* Vol. 27, Summer 1999, pp. 49–65.

Sandhoff, Michelle, Mady Wechsler Segal, and David Segal, "Gender Issues in the Transformation to an All-Volunteer Force: A Transnational Perspective," in Stuart Cohen, ed., *The New Citizen Armies: Israel's Armed Forces in Comparative Perspective,* New York: Routledge, 2010, pp. 111–131.

Schulker, David, *Three Essays on Obstacles to Improving Demographic Representation in the Armed Forces*, Santa Monica, Calif.: RAND Corporation, RGSD-274, 2010. As of July 19, 2017:
https://www.rand.org/pubs/rgs_dissertations/RGSD274.html

Secretary of the U.S. Air Force, "2015 Diversity and Inclusion (D&I) Initiatives," memorandum to all airmen, Washington, D.C., March 4, 2015a. As of August 31, 2017: http://www.af.mil/Portals/1/documents/SECAF/FINALDiversity_Inclusion_Memo2.pdf

———, "Air Force Diversity and Inclusion," memorandum to all airmen, Washington, D.C., March 4, 2015b. As of August 31, 2017: http://www.af.mil/Portals/1/documents/SECAF/FINALDiversity_Inclusion_Memo1.pdf

———, "Fact Sheet: 2016 Diversity and Inclusion Initiatives," Washington, D.C., September 30, 2016. As of September 1, 2017: http://www.af.mil/Portals/1/documents/diversity/Attach2_2016%20Diversity%20and%20Inclusion%20Initatives%20Fact%20Sheet.pdf?ver=2016-09-30-111307-623

Segal, Mady Wechsler, "The Military and the Family as Greedy Institutions," *Armed Forces & Society,* Vol. 13, No.1, 1986, p. 9.

———, "Women's Military Roles Cross-Nationally: Past, Present, and Future," *Gender and Society*, Vol. 9, 1995, pp. 757–775.

Segal, Mady Wechsler, and David R. Segal, "Social Change and the Participation of Women in the American Military," in Louis Kriesberg, ed., *Research in Social Movements, Conflicts and Change*, Greenwich, Conn.: JAI Press, Vol. 5, pp. 235–258, 1983.

Segal, Mady Wechsler, David R. Segal, Jerald G. Bachman, Peter Freedman-Doan, and Patrick M. O'Malley, "Gender and the Propensity to Enlist in the U.S. Military," *Gender Issues,* Summer 1998, pp. 65–87.

Segal, Mady Wechsler, Meridith Hill Thanner, and David R. Segal, "Hispanic and African American Men and Women in the U.S. Military: Trends in Representation," *Race, Gender and Class,* Vol. 14, No. 3-4, 2007, pp. 48–64.

Shaffer, Margaret A., David A. Harrison, K. Matthew Gilley, Dora M. Luk, "Struggling for Balance Amid Turbulence on International Assignments: Work-Family Conflict, Support and Commitment," *Journal of Management*, Vol. 27, 2001, pp. 99–121.

Smith, David G., and Judith E. Rosenstein, "Gender and the Military Profession Early Career Influences, Attitudes, and Intentions," *Armed Forces & Society*, Vol. 43(2), 2017, pp. 260–279.

U.S. Air Force, homepage, undated. As of July 19, 2017: http://www.af.mil/Diversity.aspx

U.S. Department of Defense, "The Uniformed Services Blended Retirement System," web page, undated. As of July 20, 2017: http://militarypay.defense.gov/BlendedRetirement/

———, *2015 Demographics: Profile of the Military Community*, 2015a, pp. 1–193. As of April 10, 2017:
http://download.militaryonesource.mil/12038/MOS/Reports/2015-Demographics-Report.pdf

———, "Fact Sheet: Building the First Link to the Force of the Future," Washington, D.C., 2015b. As of July 21, 2016:
http://www.defense.gov/Portals/1/features/2015/0315_force-of-the-future/documents/FotF_Fact_Sheet_-_FINAL_11.18.pdf

———, "Fact Sheet: Building the Second Link to the Force of the Future Strengthening Comprehensive Family Benefit," Washington, D.C., 2016a. As of July 21, 2016:
http://www.defense.gov/Portals/1/Documents/pubs/Fact_Sheet_Tranche_2_FOTF_FINAL.pdf

———, "Fact Sheet: The Next Two Links to the Force of the Future," Washington, D.C., 2016b. As of July 21, 2016:
http://www.defense.gov/Portals/1/features/2015/0315_force-of-the-future/Fact-Sheet-The-Next-Two-Links-to-the-Force-of-the-Future.pdf

U. S. Government Accountability Office, *Military Personnel: DoD Should Develop a Plan to Evaluate the Effectiveness of Its Career Intermission Pilot Program,* Washington, D.C., GAO 16-35, October 2015.